Henry Craik

The Hebrew Language

Its History and Characteristics

Henry Craik

The Hebrew Language
Its History and Characteristics

ISBN/EAN: 9783337084776

Printed in Europe, USA, Canada, Australia, Japan

Cover: Foto ©Thomas Meinert / pixelio.de

More available books at **www.hansebooks.com**

THE HEBREW LANGUAGE:

Its History and Characteristics.

INCLUDING IMPROVED RENDERINGS OF SELECT

PASSAGES IN

OUR AUTHORIZED TRANSLATION

OF THE

OLD TESTAMENT.

BY HENRY CRAIK.

PREFACE.

THE design of the following pages, is to aid in diffusing, among Christians in general, a measure of information relative to the external History and exact interpretation of the Holy Scriptures. I am very desirous that this little work should not be regarded as intended merely, or even chiefly, for those who are acquainted with the Original Languages. I am not without hope that the facts and criticisms which it contains may be found useful even to those who may have made some progress in acquaintance with Hebrew or Greek; but I have mainly had in view the instruction of that large class of intelligent readers of our English Bible who are disposed to welcome any work likely to assist them in the study of that precious volume.

About one-third of the whole was written several years since; and, in the form of Lectures, was publicly delivered in different places, both in England

and Scotland. It was also, some time ago, submitted to the critical judgment of the very accomplished Dean of Westminster, then Professor in King's College, London. I may say, that he very courteously consented to peruse the manuscript, and afterwards favoured me with a kind note, in which he expressed himself approvingly of its contents. His approval, however, must not be understood as if it committed him to any responsibility in reference to my remarks on points of Old Testament criticism, inasmuch as, amidst the extent and variety of his other labours, he does not profess to have found leisure for the exact cultivation of Hebrew learning.

I may add, that having for several years past enjoyed the privilege of occasionally corresponding with some of the most distinguished of our Biblical scholars, I have found that a common interest in sacred studies has a very powerful effect in promoting Christian fellowship, even between those who have never had any opportunity of personal intercourse. Such fellowship may surely be regarded as, in some measure, an earnest of that time when we shall no longer see through a glass darkly, but shall know even as we are known.

Besides the Appendix, intended to illustrate more fully certain matters briefly referred to in the text of the book, I have added a distinct essay on the subject of Biblical Revision. The facts and suggestions therein given are the fruit of habitual study of the Original Scriptures, and of considerable reflection on the points involved in the question at issue.

The Work, although so small, involves altogether a great variety of particulars, and (besides errors of the Press, which, I am sorry to say, in some instances, were not detected until the sheets were printed off) may possibly be found to contain some statements not perfectly accurate. I shall esteem it a great kindness if any scholar, skilled in such studies, would be so kind as to point out to me any errors which he may meet with. As I desire nothing but truth, I shall thankfully welcome candid criticism from whatever quarter it may come. Should it please God that a Second Edition be required, such criticism may be of essential service in aiding me in seeking to make that Edition an improvement upon the present.

I think it right to mention that, in saving me the labour of transcription, and in the translation of the

extract from Schultens, given in Appendix C., as
well as in revising the proof sheets, &c., I have
obtained valuable assistance from my learned and
laborious friend, Mr. W. ELFE TAYLER, the Author
of many works on subjects connected with
Theological study, and whose recent publication on
"The History of the Pope's Temporal Power," is
calculated to furnish most seasonable information
in relation to matters fitted to excite very deep
interest, both among Roman Catholics and Protestants.
I heartily commend its details to all who feel alive to
the importance of the present crisis in the history of
Romanism.

I would request the reader to correct, with his pen
the following misprints—

PAGE 41.—Joshua—Jehovah—Salvation, should be
              Joshua=Jehovah-Salvation.
   —   Matthew v. 21, should be Matthew i. 21.

CONTENTS.

APPENDIX.

APPENDIX.

CHAPTER I.

Introductory Remarks.

THE object of the present work is two-fold. In the *First* place, to furnish such information relative to the Hebrew Language as may be found interesting to Christians in general; *Secondly*, to advocate its claims upon the attention of such as may have leisure, opportunity, and inclination to pursue the study of it.

In following out this two-fold object,—

I.—I would endeavour to lay before the reader a Brief Sketch of the History of Hebrew Philology—accompanied with a notice of the principal sources of information relative to the meaning of its radical words.

II.—I would attempt to point out and illustrate some of the leading Characteristics of the Language.

B

III.—I would offer some observations on the benefits
connected with a knowledge of Hebrew;
and the spirit and temper of mind in which
the study should be pursued.

There are one or two remarks, of a preliminary
nature, which may aid in securing the attention of
the reader.

It is well known, that some excellent Christians
are disposed to shrink back, with a kind of sensitive
timidity, or dislike, from any public reference to the
original languages of the Scriptures; and, particularly
object to any proposed alterations of the English
Bible. I would desire to *respect* the scruples, while
I am unable to *defer to the judgment,* of such
individuals.

Let it be fully admitted that the Authorized
Version is, on the whole, *admirably* executed; that
it is perfectly adequate for the instruction of the
believing reader in all the leading essential verities
of our holy faith; that it furnishes a far more faithful
representation of the Hebrew Original than either
the Greek Septuagint, or the Latin Vulgate; and that,
in fine, when regarded as a whole, it may be looked
upon as superior to any other English Translation.
Let it, moreover, be firmly maintained, that a lowly
heart and a dependent, prayerful frame of spirit are
of infinitely more importance, for enabling the reader
to profit by the perusal of the Scriptures, than the
possession of the profoundest learning, apart from

spirituality of mind and rectitude of purpose; and that a prayerful reading of the English Translation will secure, for the humble and unlettered disciple, a higher degree of attainment in Divine knowledge, than can be acquired through the aid of unsanctified learning, however profound or extensive. In short, let those who cannot read the original languages of Scripture, and are not so situated as to be able to acquire them, be satisfied and thankful, that they can read, *in their own tongue*, the wonderful works of God; and let them prize the privilege of a Translated Bible, as one of their choicest blessings. On the other hand, no unprejudiced person, capable of judging, can refuse to acknowledge, that there *are* certain *secondary*, yet *important* advantages attendant upon a knowledge of those languages, in which the Scriptures of the Old and New Testaments were originally written.

These advantages may be illustrated by a reference to a parallel case, connected with the things of the present life. Were I to receive from some near and valued relative, who had resided for a very long time in some foreign country, a communication written in a language which I did not understand, I should thankfully avail myself of the help of a faithful translator. But, supposing I were afterwards enabled to acquire the language, with what increased interest and satisfaction should I peruse the letter in the original! The satisfaction I should experience would

be very much in proportion to the importance I
might attach to the subject of the communication.
Supposing a rich relation were to die in a distant
country, and leave his last will and testament written
in some foreign tongue, would not most of those to
whom property had been left, and who valued the
possession of earthly riches, deeply regret their
inability to understand the language which their
wealthy relative had chosen to employ in the composition of so important a document? And shall the
men of the world be more interested in the last will
and testament of a wealthy relative, than Christians
are found to be in reference to the meaning of that
book which describes their heavenly inheritance, and
contains the record of the "exceedingly great and
precious promises?"

AGAIN: there may be some who are disposed to
regard the subject of this little work as suited only
for *students.* To what purpose, say they, should we
occupy ourselves with a work on Hebrew, inasmuch
as we are altogether unacquainted with that ancient
language, and are never likely to apply ourselves to
the study of it? Now I would just remind such
persons, that there are *many* subjects, respecting
which it is important that we should have *some* information, although we never intend thoroughly to
investigate them. Most educated persons have
some slight acquaintance with astronomy, mechanics,
geology, &c., &c., in their results, though they may

never have attempted to make themselves masters of those branches of science. In a similar way, it may be affirmed that there are many facts relative to the language of the Old Testament, that have a measure of interest for all intelligent believers in Divine revelation.

How many interesting enquiries may suggest themselves to the mind of a reflecting, but ill-informed reader of our Authorized version! The title-page informs him, that the English Translation of the Old Testament was made from the original tongue, and the dedication to King James, still retained in the ordinary editions, may lead him to infer that this Translation was first published in the early part of the Seventeenth century. But whence, he may enquire, did the Translators obtain *their* knowledge of the Hebrew Original? How were they able definitely to determine the meaning of its vocables? Did they servilely follow the guidance of previous Translators? Did they proceed on grounds of plausible conjecture, or on principles of moral certainty? Such an individual may have *heard* of the existence of Hebrew Lexicons, as books that explain the meaning of Hebrew terms; but whence did the authors of such works obtain their information? Do all such authorities agree in their testimony? And, if they differ, what occasions this diversity? And on what grounds are the statements of *one* writer to be judged preferable to those of *another?*

Such are some of the leading questions that may suggest themselves to a reflecting reader. Consider the importance of such enquiries to those who are resting their prospects for eternity on the assumption that the representation of what the Original Scriptures contain, as given in the English Version, is substantially correct; and it will be acknowledged that, just in so far as any individual is imbued with a devout reverence for the Divine oracles, so will he be interested in those questions that relate to their exact interpretation. May I not, therefore, reasonably expect to carry along with me the thoughtful attention of the reader, while—in tracing the History of Hebrew Philology, and in expounding the mode in which the meaning of its vocables has been determined—I endeavour to furnish a satisfactory solution of such enquiries as I have supposed likely to arise in the mind of an intelligent Christian, unacquainted with the facts that supply the needed information?

Perhaps the question may be suggested to the minds of some who may peruse these pages: How, amid the incessant pressure of ordinary employments, and the loud calls for the labours of Christian philanthropy, can leisure be obtained for studies of such a character? The requirements of duty must be discharged, The ignorance and vice, that are festering all around ' us, urgently demand our self-denying efforts; and is there not a danger of neglecting such calls, while devoting ourselves to the luxury of mental improvement?

There is, undoubtedly, such a danger. But, on the other hand, everything that tends to make us better acquainted with the excellencies of the Scriptures, will help us to enjoy them more fully; and the legitimate result of the richer enjoyment of Divine Truth will be to impel us more earnestly and prayerfully to seek its wider diffusion. Every Christian must see to it that he keep up devotional reading of the Bible, and secret intercourse with God in prayer, meditation, and thanksgiving. He may not warrantably neglect the duties of his position in society. He may not entirely keep himself aloof from the labours and the delights of Christian philanthropy. But, without these calls being neglected, many hours may still be husbanded—from *trivial occupations, unprofitable visiting,* and *needless sleep* — for the pursuit of such knowledge as may aid the apprehension and the enjoyment of the Divine Testimonies. Generally speaking, those who are pre-eminently studious will not be prominent in outward service; while those whose qualifications and dispositions lead them to devote themselves to outward service, will not become distinguished for their studious habits, or their eminent attainments. Yet, I apprehend, although not always *apparently* the most successful, *he* will be found to be the happiest and most useful Christian, who seeks to combine, in some measure, the labours of the philanthropist and the scholar, and who, while active in the discharge of external duties, is diligent also in the labours of studious retirement.

CHAPTER II.

History of the Hebrew Language down to the Commencement of the Middle Ages.

I now proceed briefly to sketch the history of Hebrew Philology:—

The grounds upon which the ancient Hebrew may be regarded as the Primitive Language of our race are of very great weight, and have been repeatedly brought forward in works adapted to the general reader. I do not therefore intend to dwell at any length upon this part of my subject. I would merely remark, that no other known language can furnish *equal* evidence of so remote an antiquity. It would be altogether out of the question to compare in this respect, the Latin, or Greek, with the Hebrew. The Sanscrit, or Chinese, might urge their claims on grounds of much greater plausibility; but I am not aware that any scholars, adequate to form a correct judgment, would affirm that the claims of either will bear investigation, or can be established on grounds of historical certainty. The Hebrew belongs to what is generally called the Shemitic family of languages, all of which were doubtless originally one, and in course of time diverged into several dialects. Of those the most important, besides the Hebrew, are the Chaldee, Syriac and Arabic.

The evidence for the antiquity of the Biblical Hebrew is of an obvious character. In perusing the writings of Moses, in the original, we find a correspondency between the names appropriated to persons, and the circumstances under which the names were given, that is not to be found in any other language. *The proper names in the Book of Genesis carry along with them a significance in the Hebrew which is lost to the mere reader of a translation.* This can only be satisfactorily accounted for, on the assumption that the language, in which Moses wrote, was substantially the same as that which had been spoken from the beginning of the world.

There is no reason for supposing that the language of Noah was materially different from that which had been spoken in Paradise by our first parents: neither is it at all likely, that the sons of Noah would substitute another form of speech, in place of that to which they had been habituated from their earliest youth. And still further, we may infer that the language of Moses, as exhibited in the Pentateuch, did not substantially differ from that which had been employed by Adam and the Antediluvian Patriarchs. There is, therefore, no good reason for supposing that the

primitive language was totally lost at the confusion
of tongues. Those who were engaged in the erection
of the Tower of Babel had *their* form of speech so
affected, that they could no longer understand one
another; but this would only apply to those who
were actually engaged in that audacious enterprise.
There was probably a godly remnant who stood aloof
from that rebellious effort at aggrandizement, and
retained, in consequence, their primitive tongue.
Such are some of the most obvious and convincing
reasons tending to establish the substantial identity
between the Hebrew of the Old Testament, and the
primitive language of the human family.

With such slight modifications as almost all languages undergo through the lapse of ages, the
primitive Hebrew continued a living language, at
least down to the period of the Babylonish Captivity.
At what period the pure dialect ceased to be vernacular, cannot with certainty be determined. Some
maintain that, during their residence in the country
of their captivity, the Jews adopted the dialect of
their conquerors, and that thus the Chaldee was
substituted for the language of the ancient Patriarchs.
This, I suppose, is the commonly received opinion;
but there are some strong reasons which make me
hesitate to adopt it. The prophets Zechariah and
Malachi addressed themselves to their countrymen in
Hebrew. Is it likely that they would have been led
to employ a form of speech which, like the Latin

during the middle ages, had become unintelligible to the great mass of the people? At whatever period the ancient Hebrew fell into desuetude among the bulk of the community, there can be no question but, that at the time of Christ, a Syro-Chaldaic dialect prevailed in Judea.

This fact appears evident from the specimens of the language then spoken, which have been preserved in the writings of the Evangelists and Apostles. It would seem to have been a compound of the Chaldee, (or Eastern Aramæan), with the Syriac, (or Western Aramæan); both of which, as mentioned above, were closely connected with the Hebrew. It would be interesting to collect together all the instances of this compound dialect that are to be found in the New Testament; and to compare each particular example with the corresponding expression in the earlier form of the language. This, however, would far exceed the limits of the present work. Still it may be desirable, at the close of the work, to refer to some of these, in connexion with the passages of Scripture in which they occur.* But although—as these passages will convince the reader—the dialect in use when our blessed Lord appeared on earth was very different from that employed by Moses and the Prophets, still, the Biblical Hebrew continued to be cultivated by the Literati among the Jewish people.

* Appendix (A.)

After the times of the Apostles, and during the early centuries of the Christian Church, the knowledge of the Hebrew Scriptures was almost entirely confined to the Jews. The leading Christian Teachers, with the exception of Origen in the second century, and Jerome in the fourth, seem to have been entirely unacquainted with the original of the Old Testament, and to have regarded the Greek version, commonly called the Septuagint, as the authoritative standard. Exceedingly valuable from its antiquity, as that version may unquestionably be considered, it is nevertheless disfigured by almost innumerable blunders and mistranslations. Let any competent scholar read the fifty-third of Isaiah, in the Septuagint, and compare the Greek Translation of that chapter with the original Hebrew, and he will perceive, most distinctly, the superiority of the latter. The doctrine of a propitiatory sacrifice—the central truth of the Christian system—is clearly and unmistakeably taught in the Hebrew; that doctrine is very much obscured in the 9th and 10th verses of the Greek version.* This is the more remarkable, inasmuch as the Hebrew Bible was in the hands of the enemies of the Gospel; while the Septuagint was the standard of authority among Christians. The mistranslation of the Seventy, in this instance, becomes important, as an incidental proof that the Christians, on the one

* See Appendix (B.)

hand, did not alter the Greek version to make it speak in accordance with Christianity; and that the Jews, on the other hand, did not dare to alter the language of the prophet, so as to obscure the doctrine of a propitiatory sacrifice.

Had the Greek Translation clearly expressed the doctrine of the Christian Scriptures, while the Hebrew original less distinctly taught it, the Jews might have alleged, with some show of plausibility, that Christians had accommodated the version of the Prophet, so as to suit the doctrines which they had received from the New Testament. How satisfactory it is to find, that the Hebrew Scriptures themselves bear the clearest testimony to the doctrine of the Christian Atonement! Every fresh illustration of this vital truth is welcome to the heart of the believer in Jesus. Without this truth, there is no repose nor refreshment for the weary spirit. A Gospel, without a propitiatory sacrifice, fails to meet the necessities of a sinful creature; fails to manifest the attributes of God; fails to reveal the links of that golden chain, which serves at once to unite the children of Adam to God, and to each other. Apart from this truth;

> Learning is dull to us, pleasure is vain;

Neither can

> The golden idols that deceive the world,
> Ambition, glory, riches, fame, applause—

minister to the heart such calm and satisfying enjoyment, as may be derived from a single half-hour's believing meditation on the love of Him who laid down His life on the Cross for sinners!

Some of the leading Christian teachers—the distinguished Augustine among the rest—appear to have regarded the Seventy Translators as having been *inspired*. This baseless fancy has been lately revived, and advocated with considerable ingenuity by a modern theologian, in a work entitled "An Apology for the Septuagint." *Inspired* translators could not have been permitted to fall into the errors which abound in this ancient Version; and very few persons of sound judgment—moderately conversant with the facts of the case—would yield their assent to so groundless an hypothesis.

CHAPTER III.

State of Hebrew Learning during the Middle Ages, down to the Early portion of the Eighteenth Century.

DURING the long and dreary period of the dark ages almost every species of solid learning was neglected throughout Christendom, and Hebrew found scarcely a single cultivator among the few Christian scholars, scattered here and there, throughout the European nations, like stars in a cloudy sky. Yet amongst that people who were not "reckoned among the nations"—whose hearts refused to receive Him of whom "Moses in the law and the Prophets did write,"—there was preserved the knowledge of the Hebrew Scriptures—those very writings which contained the germ of Christianity, and the evidence that Jesus of Nazareth was indeed the Messiah promised unto the fathers. In the twelfth century, Raymond, a monk of the Dominican order, attempted to revive the study of Hebrew in the Church, and in 1311, Pope Clement the fifth published a decree, requiring that, in every University in Christendom, there should be appointed six professors of Hebrew and the cognate dialects; but, for the space of two centuries, it was found impossible to provide a single professor in any University with the exception of Oxford. Seldom have the Papal decrees aimed at objects so blameless and beneficial; but even the power of the Popedom in its palmiest days could not secure the appointment of qualified teachers— when none were to be found within the pale of Christendom.

In 1506—at the early dawn of the Reformation— John Reuchlin compiled the first dictionary and grammar of any real value, excepting such as had, at an earlier period, been composed by the Jewish grammarians. This eminent scholar may be regarded as the *founder of Hebrew Philology and Lexicography among Christians*. Immediately afterwards, the general revival of learning gave a new impulse to the study of the ancient Scriptures. From the time of Reuchlin, the names of distinguished Hebraists appear, either as cotemporaries, or in rapid succession, on the page of literary history. Among these, the two Buxtorfs, father and son, deserve to occupy a very prominent place. Luther's eminence, as a Reformer, has almost cast into the shade his high attainments as a scholar; otherwise, his name would legitimately occupy a distinguished position among those who devoted themselves to the study of the Hebrew Bible. He himself tells us, that, "*limited as was the measure of his attainments in the knowledge of the sacred language, he would not exchange what he did possess for all the treasures of the Universe.*" This was the deliberate and recorded judgment of one of the most eminent servants of God ever given to the Church of Christ.

Among the other eminent men of learning, who devoted themselves to this study, may be enumerated the following:—Fabricius Capito, Conrad Pellican, Sebastian Munster, John Forster, Avenarius, Schindler, Marius de Calasio, Neumann, Loescher, Bohlius, and Cocceius. But time would fail me to recall the names and achievements of those who, about the time of the Great Reformation, and after that memorable deliverance, devoted the energies of their minds to the pursuit of sacred studies. The names of most of them are now scarcely ever mentioned ; their writings, for the most part, are neglected and forgotten. But if they, through the knowledge of the letter, penetrated into the hidden meaning of the divine testimonies, they have not lost their reward. Their labours brought along with them a *present* satisfaction, and ensured a *future* recompense. I would only add the names of Bochart, Leigh, Castel, Robertson, Lightfoot, and Pococke—the first of the list being a French Protestant, the other five being our own countrymen.

CHAPTER IV.

Progress of Hebrew Learning down to the Present Time.

COMING down to a later period—the early part of the eighteenth century—we reach the period at which Albert Schultens was raised up to give a fresh impetus to the study of the Old Testament. When that very distinguished scholar began to devote the powers of his penetrating genius and the resources of his capacious mind to the promotion of sacred learning, he found that very much remained to be accomplished in order to the complete elucidation of the sacred tongue. The signification of the far greater number of words which make up its vocabulary was matter of ascertained knowledge; but there remained several terms the force of which was matter of entire uncertainty; a good many others about the meaning of which there was considerable ground for doubt; and a still larger number, respecting which it had to be acknowledged, that whilst their *general import* was well understood, their *primary* or *ideal* meaning was unknown. The mode in which the defective information might be successfully enquired after had, previously to his time, been matter of diligent investigation and earnest controversy; and, in connexion with the further history of Hebrew Philology, it may be interesting to be furnished with a brief account of some of the various theories which were started in reference to the important enquiry, as to the 'way in which the meaning of unknown or doubtful words might be satisfactorily determined.

Let me first, however, recall to the reader's mind the deep interest connected with such an investigation. On the correct rendering of *one single term*, the whole force and bearing of a passage of Scripture may depend. The correctness of any such rendering must depend upon the soundness of the principles according to which the meaning of the particular term has been determined; and if any given number of Hebrew words should have a false meaning assigned them, the passages of Scripture wherein those words happen to occur must be either obscured or perverted by inaccurate translation. How deeply important, then, is the enquiry relative to the principles on which we are warranted to decide, in doubtful instances, the exact meaning of the words employed in the Hebrew Scriptures!

Some learned men maintained, that the Septuagint translation was to be taken as the authoritative

standard by which to ascertain the meaning of
doubtful terms; others upheld the authority of the
Latin Vulgate; whilst a third class of critics looked
up to the Rabbinical writers, as furnishing the only
true key to the interpretation of the Old Testament.
Others, who took a more comprehensive view of the
subject, proposed to call in the aid of *all* the ancient
versions, and thus to enjoy the advantage of several
distinct and independent witnesses. The celebrated
Forster, who flourished about the middle of the
sixteenth century, dissatisfied with the theories
advocated by other scholars, and especially indignant
at the thought of Christians being required to learn
at the feet of Jewish Rabbis, propounded an hypothesis of his own. He maintained that, from the
Hebrew Bible itself—without the aid of the ancient
Versions, or that of the Jewish teachers—the exact
knowledge of the language was to be obtained.
According to this singular notion, the Hebrew Bible
was to be dealt with in a similar way to the mode
employed in deciphering a MS. written in some unknown character. There is an art by which, supposing
the *language* to be intelligible to the reader, an unknown *character* may be deciphered. But it would
be altogether miraculous, were any one to arrive at
the knowledge of a *language previously unknown*,
without any help from grammars, or dictionaries, or
cognate dialects, or assistance from such as already
understood it.

Avenarius may be regarded as a follower of
Forster. The metaphysical Bohlius undertook to
demonstrate, *a priori*, the exact signification of the
words employed in the Hebrew Scriptures; or, to use
his own language, "to extract the universal and
abstract signification of the radical terms out of the
bowels of the sacred Scriptures solely by the aid of
assiduity and acuteness." Similar to the above
hypothesis was that of Gussetius, who maintained,
that, just in the same way as the sun shines by its
own light, so the Hebrew Bible contains, within
itself, the evidence of its own meaning. Lastly, I
would notice the theory of Neumann and Loescher,
which for a while obtained some credit, that the
letters of the Hebrew alphabet severally denoted
certain ideas, and, that the combination of the ideas
inherent in the three letters of which any root was
composed made up the radical signification of that
particular root.

It is unnecessary to occupy the reader's attention
in minutely investigating and exposing such unfounded speculations. It would be sad, indeed, to be
under the necessity of resting the interpretation of the
Old Testament upon such unsatisfactory grounds.

Previously to the period at which Schultens
flourished, the kindred Oriental dialects had begun to
be cultivated in Europe, and those who had devoted
themselves to such studies found that thence fresh
aid was to be derived for the elucidation of the

ancient Hebrew. Schultens took up this discovery
with earnestness, assiduity, and zeal. He studied—
and with almost unparalleled success—the cognate
languages. In an incredibly short space of time, he
obtained an extraordinary knowledge of the Arabic;
and then applied the knowledge of that language to
the determining the signification of those terms the
exact import of which had previously been un-
ascertained. But, while he gave great prominence to
the cognate dialects, and particularly to the Arabic,
as important helps, he did not discard the aid of
those other sources of information which the
providence of God had left open. According to
Schultens—and what qualified scholar would refuse
to agree with him?—there are, at least, *five* or *six*
sources whence important aid may be derived. The
ancient versions; the testimony of the Rabbinical
writers; the kindred dialects; the exigence of the
context; the comparison of parallel passages; the
correspondency between certain letters;—may all be
considered as so many distinct auxiliaries, in enabling
us, on principles of moral certainty, to determine
or verify the exact force or general import of
particular radical terms.*

Schultens may have carried his partiality for the
Arabic too far; some of his explanations, thence
derived, may be questionable; but, unlike some men

of eminent attainments, he was equally distinguished
for *comprehensiveness*, and *acuteness* of mind. His
writings manifest a devout reverence for the Divine
oracles; an earnest love of truth; a power of penetrating perception; soundness of judgment; large
mental resources; and a fine enthusiasm for sacred
learning that must have exerted a powerful corresponding influence upon young and ardent minds.
His *Origines Hebraeae*, his *Vetus et Regia Via
Hebraizandi*, his Philological *Commentaries on Job*
and the *Book of Proverbs*, remain as monuments of
his diligence, piety, and unrivalled erudition. *He*
led the way, and *others* have followed in his track. No
modern Lexicographer would revive, or maintain, the
fanciful speculations which, previous to the time of
Schultens, prevailed so extensively among sacred
philologists; and Gesenius himself—perhaps the
greatest of our modern Lexicographers—may, in some
respects, be regarded as having reached his eminent
position through carrying out the principles which
his distinguished predecessor had promulgated and
defended. Instead of contending for the *sole
authority* of any *one* source of information, relative
to the force of disputed terms, Hebrew Lexicographers
are now agreed in having recourse to them all. It
surely becomes us thankfully to avail ourselves of
every legitimate mode of satisfactorily determining the
meaning of those Divine utterances, which, "holy
men of old spake as they were moved by the Holy
Ghost."

If any of my readers were previously uninformed respecting the points to which I have directed their attention in the foregoing pages, they will now be in some measure competent to answer the enquiries suggested above, relative to the sources of information respecting the meaning of Hebrew terms, and the principles according to which their signification may be determined. The true rendering of Hebrew words depends, not upon conjecture, but upon evidence ; and that evidence is of so satisfactory a character, as, in most cases, to produce the confidence of moral certainty.

The result of the labours bestowed by ancient and modern philologists, on the elucidation of the Hebrew language, may be found perhaps most fully in the well-known Lexicon of Gesenius. I must, however, add one word respecting his theology, It cannot be denied, and it ought not to be concealed, that Gesenius was defective in reverence for those very Scriptures to the elucidation of which he devoted the labours of a lifetime and that he was unhappily imbued with the rationalistic sentiments so common among German theologians. For this reason, his works need to be read with caution. An admirable translation of his Lexicon has been published by Bagster, and the careful revisal to which that edition has been subjected, by a faithful and orthodox translator—my learned friend, Dr. Tregelles, of Plymouth—exceedingly enhances the practical value of the work. It is to be hoped that, for English students, this edition will soon supersede every other; and that thus the excellencies of the original work may be enjoyed, without any peril being incurred, by the unestablished Christian, from the incorrect and even scoffing remarks that now and then obtrude themselves on the notice of the reader. Having been, for several years past, in the habit of using Bagster's edition of Gesenius, I can confidently recommend so valuable a help to the study of the Old Testament Scriptures to all who feel interested in the pursuit or the promotion of sacred learning.*

In writing this sketch of Hebrew Philology, the works of Loescher and Schultens have been my chief sources of information; but, as both of these authors have written in Latin, the deeply interesting facts and criticisms which they contain are inaccessible to the English reader. I would also acknowledge my obligations to a very able German writer, who has written a very learned introduction to the new edition of Buxtorf's Concordance, of part of which introduction a translation appeared, some years ago, in an American periodical. Without at all desiring to detract from the learning and ability of the treatise referred to, I may just take this opportunity of guarding inexperienced readers against taking their impression of the views of Schultens from the representations of

* Appendix (D).

that work. My conviction of the substantial value of the views maintained by that admirable philologist has already been given. I ask no one, capable of testing the point for himself, to take *my* judgment, any more than to submit it to the decision of the writer referred to. But let only his briefest treatise— his *Vetus et Regia Via Hebraizandi*—*(i.e.,* "The ancient and royal mode of studying the Hebrew language")— be appealed to, and the excellencies of this matchless scholar will shine forth with a lustre that must overpower all the opposition of those who would detract from his reputation. His writings have never—so far as I know—been presented in an English dress ; and the limited demand for such works in this country operates as a prohibition upon any prudent bookseller from incurring the risk of publishing a translation. But to the Christian scholar, his flowing periods—reminding one of the majestic language of Cicero—furnish at once gratification for the taste, information for the understanding, and profitable instruction for the heart.

And now, in concluding this branch of my subject, let me pause to enquire how the reader is affected by the necessarily rapid and imperfect sketch which has been brought before him? Ought not the past history and present position of Hebrew Philology to excite lively gratitude to the Giver of every good and perfect gift, not only for the bestowment, but for the preservation of the sacred volume? Had the knowledge of Hebrew been once entirely lost, (and such *might* have been the case), it could never—except by miracle—have been restored. So far from having been lost, we may affirm, without fear of contradiction, that, at no period since it ceased to be a spoken language, has it been more scientifically studied than during the last and the present century. It may be safely affirmed, that Hebrew has been more thoroughly investigated since the early part of the eighteenth century, than it had ever been for, at least, two thousand years before. It carries along with it the venerable dignity of age, while it retains the vigour and energy of youth.

There is something imposing and affecting, to a thoughtful mind, in the view of any object of very remote antiquity. Antiquarian tendencies—ridiculous when carried to an extreme—are deeply seated in the nature of our mysterious humanity. We should become neither better nor happier beings by uprooting them, even if that were possible. That utilitarianism which boasts of superiority to such weaknesses and prejudices is inimical to the higher interests of man. Who would wish to gaze, without elevated emotion, on Melrose or Tintern? All thoughtful minds regard with feelings of solemnity and reverence the memorials of bygone ages—the ruins of a monastery, an abbey, or a baronial castle. We think of the multitudes that once trod the deserted floor, and whose voices once echoed through the silent walls, and the grey ruins become sublime, through association with the hoary antiquity

of other days. On the same principle—to a religious
mind—how venerable an object is a copy of the Hebrew
Scriptures! As you open it, the page exhibits the
very words that Moses, and David, and Isaiah,
uttered; and those words convey, to the instructed
reader, the very thoughts that filled their minds.
How wonderful, that the language in which the
patriarch Job expressed his resignation, and poured
forth his complainings, should, after the lapse of
perhaps *four thousand years*, be still read, and
understood, and enjoyed! And then again, how
cheering to think of the value of those utterances
which came forth mysteriously prompted by the
Divine Spirit! and of the thousands, and tens of
thousands, who, in meditating over them, have
found enlightenment, consolation, and joy!

What a subject for serious reflection is a Hebrew
Bible! How many minds have devoted themselves
to the investigation of its meaning! How many
have looked upon its characters and found the page
to them entirely meaningless; and resolved, that, by
the help of God, and by dint of honourable toil, they
would make that page give forth its hidden significance! How many have cleared away the initiatory
difficulties, and rejoiced to find light breaking in
upon their path! How many have become so
familiar with the ancient language of the patriarchs,
as to prefer it to the accents of their own mother
tongue? How many have felt a force, a tenderness,

a sublimity in the language of David, which led them to prefer the Hebrew Psalter above all the specimens of Sacred Song! And if the course of time runs on, how many ingenuous minds will yet find themselves inwardly impelled to the study of these holy oracles; and will become the instruments of guiding, and assisting, the studies of their successors in the same field of inquiry! The acquisition of the ancient Hebrew is not to be attained by the labour of a few months, or even of a few years. The longer we pursue the study of it, the more will fresh fields for investigation open upon our view; whilst in pushing onward our peaceful conquests, we shall not be left to weep, like Macedonia's madman, that there are no more worlds to be subdued. He who seeks to make solid acquisitions must gird himself for vigorous exertion, and adopt as his motto, the energetic language of the poet:—

> Toiling, rejoicing, sorrowing,
>   Onward thro' life he goes,
> Each morning sees some task begun,
>   Each evening sees its close;
> Something attempted, something done,
>   Has earned a night's repose.

CHAPTER V.

On the Leading Characteristics of the Hebrew Language.

I COME now to the exposition of some of the *leading characteristics* of the ancient Hebrew. As the glassy lake reflects the image of external nature, so language may be regarded as the mirror of intelligent mind; and just as the surface of the lake reflects, with equal faithfulness, the tiniest shrub that grows upon its banks, and the dread magnificence of the starry firmament, so language serves alike to express the feeble conceptions of early childhood, and to give forth the thoughts and purposes of Jehovah. The history of any form of speech is, to a greater or less extent, the record of thought and feeling; and the record of thought and feeling constitutes the history of humanity.

There are various external circumstances upon which the characteristic features of any given language may be said to depend; various types and models, according to which, the several languages employed by the various tribes of the human family, have been moulded and conformed. *Climate* is one of those external circumstances. The general results of climate may, according to the ingenious Loescher, be summed up in the following couplet:—

> "The Western tongues *flow on*, the Eastern *leap*;
> The Southern *run*, the sluggish Northern *creep*."

These several characteristic qualities may be mingled *in diverse proportions*, according to the locality, and other modifying circumstances.

Thus, of the Western tongues, the Greek has more vivacity than the Latin; Greece lying south-east from Italy. The Latin, as most readers are aware, is distinguished for gravity and stateliness, and moves, as in the page of Cicero, with a slow, dignified, majestic step. The languages of the East, on the other hand, abound in sparkling imagery, corresponding to the ardent temperament proper to that sunny clime; while the Northern tongues correspond with the temperature of a cold and inclement sky. Thus the intonation of many natives of Scotland is slow, when contrasted with the livelier utterance of an Englishman. France, as situated to the South of England, is possessed of a still more vivacious form of speech. French—the language of superficial politeness—is rapid, lively, flowing, and well fitted to be the medium of intercourse among a polished, talkative, and thoughtless people. It is but little

adapted for elevated writing of any kind, least of all
for elevated poetry. In this respect it is far inferior
to our own. What Englishman would be willing to
surrender his mother tongue, and take in exchange
the language of our Gallic neighbours? And who
does not perceive a correspondency between the pro-
verbially frivolous and excitable character of the
French people, and the whole cast and composition of
their language? or between the masculine character
of Englishmen, and our fine old, nervous Anglo-Saxon
dialect?

The situation of Palestine—on the Eastern shore
of the Mediterranean—would lead us to infer that
the language of its people would partake of the
qualities belonging to the other Eastern dialects.
Accordingly, it is forcible, picturesque, abrupt,
delighting in figurative expressions, and abounding
in bold and impressive imagery. But, in comparison
with Persia, India, and other Oriental countries,
Palestine might almost be reckoned as belonging to
the Western world; and thus we find that the Hebrew
is characterized by the simplicity, dignity, and
gravity that distinguish the languages of the West.

This leads me to remark how greatly the influence
of climate may be modified by other circumstances.
Locality is only *one* of the several congruous, or dis-
congruous, influences that act upon the character of a
people, and mould their form of speech; and if
we would satisfactorily account for the peculiar

characteristics of any particular language, we must investigate the causes that have exerted their combined influence in imparting to it the form and features which it is found to have assumed.

In the case of the Hebrews, those causes were of the most marked and obvious nature. The early history, the civil and religious institutions of any people, naturally stamp their impress upon the national mind. If any circumstances happen to have imparted a *peculiarity of character* to a nation, this peculiarity will necessarily be developed in their language. The domestic habits, the moral principles, the general pursuits of any people, serve to colour their whole phraseology.

This may be illustrated by reference to any sect of religion, or to any school of philosophy. What observant man, who has mingled in general religious society, can have failed to recognize a peculiar mode of expression among the followers of the devoted Wesley? or among the readers of German theology? or among the disciples of any distinguished teacher? The fact that we are all exposed to such a tendency should lead us earnestly to study and devoutly to receive the instructions of Him who has commanded us to call no man master upon earth. The mannerism, into which we are all so ready to fall, is always more or less the index of weakness. How common is it to meet with individuals whose judgment concerning matters of deepest moment has been decided, not by

the testimony of Scripture, but by the authority of
eminent, energetic, devoted, but uninspired men!
John Knox and John Wesley—very different in their
mental constitution, and no less opposed to each
other in certain doctrinal opinions—have continued,
even down to the present day, to influence the
judgment, the feelings, and the phraseology of
thousands and tens of thousands. If we would give
forth before the world a fair impression of the large
and unsectarian character of Christianity, we must
guard against the habitual iteration of certain current
phrases; remembering that there is, in general, a
noble distinctness and individuality about the writers
of the Old and New Testaments. Moses, David,
Isaiah, Solomon, have, each of them, their distinct
style. Paul, and Peter, and John, all proclaim the
same Gospel, all testify to the same Saviour; yet,
how perceptible to every reader is the difference of
their mode of expression!

But to return from this long digression, let me
proceed to apply to the particular case of the Hebrew,
what has been said respecting the circumstances that
tend to modify any language. Their early history,
their sojourn in Egypt, and their deliverance from
their bondage in that country; the ceremonial
institutions; the Priesthood; the Theocracy; the
Prophetic order:—all these tended to influence the
national character, and to stamp that character upon
their form of speech.

Were the present population of France to be swept away, and the soil given over to the occupation of a people similar to the Scottish Covenanters, or to the Puritan founders of New England—supposing the substance of the language to remain—how many forms of expression, now current, would be neglected, and fall into utter desuetude, among such a people! Supposing the Puritan character to be maintained, although French should remain the language of the country, and although the influence of climate would, of course, be the same as ever, can there be any reason to doubt, that, as employed by a grave, an earnest, and a religious people, the language would become more nervous, serious, dignified? A people devoted to whatsoever things are noble, good, and true, would naturally be led so to mould and fashion their current phraseology, as that it should become the fitting vehicle for the expression of holy feeling and elevated thought.

The Patriarchs were the founders of the Jewish nation. Their walk of separation, simplicity, and godliness, required a corresponding medium of intercourse. Hence the simple dignity, the elevated seriousness, the earnest tenderness by which their language is characterized. How utterly uncalled for, among such a people, would have been many of the terms and phrases constantly employed by the present population of France! Paris—so long the centre of European luxury, and now, after repeated revolutions, the seat of *an imperial despotism*—Paris requires such a copiousness of diction as would only have encumbered the ancient Hebrews. Their manners were simple, their wants comparatively few; their thoughts, all, more or less, coloured with the religious element. These mental characteristics were reflected in their form of speech.

Having thus, by some observations on the general characteristics of languages, prepared the way for remarks of a more definite character, I would now attempt to point out more particularly some of the *Leading Characteristics of the Hebrew Tongue.*

(1.) In all languages, terms descriptive of mental states and feelings are, *in their primary import*, applicable to material objects; or, to express myself, perhaps more clearly, words, strictly and primarily representative of external objects or conditions, are employed to designate ideas belonging to the world of mind. Thus in our own language, *"to apprehend,"* in its primary signification, denotes "to lay hold of;" its application to denote an act of the mind is secondary and figurative. It is the same with the words "understand," "conceive," "recollect," "disposition," etc. Indeed, examples might be multiplied indefinitely.

There is in Hebrew a remarkable appropriateness and expressive energy in the terms employed to denote mental qualities or conditions. The original notions inherent in those terms serve to picture forth, with prominent distinctness, the mental quality which they are employed to designate. Thus, for instance, the usual term for "meek" is derived from a radical word signifying "to afflict;" thus intimating the well-known connexion ₁between *sanctified sorrow*, and the *grace of meekness.* The usual term for "wicked" comes from a root that expresses the notion of *restlessness, tumult,* or *commotion.* "There is no peace, saith my God, to the wicked." A "sinner" is one who *misses the mark;* who turns aside from his "being's end and aim"—even the favour and enjoyment of God. To "delight in" anything is radically, "to bend down" towards it, such a direction of the body being an *outward* expression of *inward* complacency. The word applied to the "law of God" (the Torah), is derived from a verb signifying "to cast," "to send out," thence "to put forth," as the hand for the purpose of giving directions, "to point out," "to indicate," "to teach." *The Law* is that which *indicates,* or *points out* to us the mind of God. "Righteousness" is properly *that which is perfectly straight.* "Truth," that which is *firm* or *stable.* "Vanity," that which is *empty.* "Anger" is derived from a root meaning *to breathe*; quick breathing being one of the external signs of irritated feeling. "To trust," is expressed, sometimes by a term meaning *to take shelter under* any object of confidence; sometimes by a word meaning *to lean upon;* in other cases by a word, the radical signification of which appears to be *to throw one's-self upon anyone*, or *to hang upon him*. Trust in God may be described, either as a putting ourselves under the shadow of his wings, a taking refuge in Him; or as a casting ourselves upon His care, a hanging in helplessness upon His Almighty strength. "To judge," is radically *to smooth, to make even, to equalise*.

The second verse of the eleventh chapter of Proverbs furnishes an apt illustration of the energy of expression resulting from combining together the ideal import of the several words that make up a sentence:—

> "When pride cometh, then cometh shame ;
> But with the lowly is wisdom."

Pride comes from a root which means "to swell;" *shame* from a word denoting "to be light, or empty;" *lowly*, from a root meaning "to chip, or smooth with a hatchet;" and *wisdom*, from a word expressing "solidity." Put these several primary significations in combination, and you get two striking images corresponding to the two divisions of the sentence:—

> "When *swelling* cometh, then cometh *lightness :*"
> "But with those who have been pruned (chipped,
> exercised by trial), there is solidity."

It may be interesting to compare the distinct, radical notions of the several terms employed respectively, in the Hebrew, Greek, and Latin, for the idea of *justice*, or *righteousness*.

The Hebrew term, as we have seen, denotes *that which is perfectly straight;* the Latin, *jus,* from jubeo, jussi, *that which is commanded;* and the Greek, δικη, *that which divides equally to all,—apportions to everyone his due.* The thought expressed by the Hebrew root is deeper than that which is conveyed either by the Latin or Greek. The Romans were a military people,—a nation of soldiers—and the idea of *rightness* was, in their minds, naturally associated with that of *obedience to orders.* The Greeks were a people foremost in all that ministers to social enjoyment and civilisation, and *their* idea of *rightness* was that which secured to all the possession of his due. The thought of an antecedent and eternal distinction between right and wrong, apart altogether from the present results of good and evil, runs through the whole system of Old Testament morality, and that thought is graphically presented to us under the image of *that which is perfectly straight.*

"Truth," again, in Hebrew, *firmness,* is in Greek *that which cannot be hid,* or that which is *unconcealed, open,* in opposition to falsehood, which lurks in the darkness. Such an instance serves to show how full of practical teaching may be the details of philology, and to remind us of our Lord's words:—

"He that doeth *truth*, cometh to the *light*."

"Truth," says the *Greek* derivation, is *that which cannot be hid.* It may be *suppressed* for a time—it may *seem* to be *buried* for ever;—but its very nature secures its ultimate revival and resurrection. The oppressor, and the persecutor, may tread it down; the bones of the martyrs may—

> "Lie scattered on the Alpine Mountains cold:"—

Their ashes may be sown—

> "O'er all the Italian fields where still doth sway
> The Triple Tyrant."

But from their ashes will grow—

> "A hundred-fold who, having learnt Christ's way,
> Early will fly the Babylonian woe."

Truth may be consumed in the person of John Huss, but must spring forth, with renewed life, in the person of Martin Luther; and neither Pope Pius IX., nor any other persecuting ruler can uproot, from the hearts of his subjects, that deep-seated apprehension of *truth* which divine grace has imparted.

The *Hebrew* derivation again reminds us of its indestructible *firmness*. The everlasting hills may tremble—the solid rocks may be shattered to atoms— the heaven and the earth may pass away—but truth remains immoveable,

> "Unhurt amidst the war of elements;
> The wreck of nature and the crash of worlds."

It will thus be seen that the study of the Hebrew language—*even as a language*—(apart from the consideration of its use, in enabling us to read the original of the Old Testament)—is full of *moral* instruction. The great Coleridge delighted to trace these ideal meanings, in his perusal of the Hebrew Scriptures; and although other languages, to a certain extent, are constructed on the same principle, yet I question whether any other form of speech contains such an amount of ethical meaning inwrought into its very framework, and pervading it as a whole.

The precious name of Jesus (in Hebrew, Jehoshua or Joshua), is derived from a root-term, that in its primary meaning, denotes "*amplitude*," "*spaciousness*." It thence was employed in the sense of "*setting at large*," "*delivering from distress*," "*saving from every kind of evil*." Let us trace this instance with some particularity:—

First, we have the root denoting:—

(1.) *To be spacious, ample, broad, wealthy, abundant, rich.*

Then (2.) *To set in a large place, to set at liberty, help, succour, aid, save.*

Then the nouns—*Deliverance, aid, safety, salvation.*

Then, prefixing the abbreviated form of Jehovah, we get the noun, *Joshua—Jehovah—Salvation,* or *Jehovah the Saviour.* How admirably this derivation illustrates the declaration of the Angel! (Matt. v. 21.)

"He shall be called Jesus, *i.e.*, Jehovah the Saviour,
    For He by Himself shall save His people from their sins."

The proper name of the most distinguished of all
the prophets, is compounded of the very same elements,
only in a different order—Jesus and Isaiah, are each
of them made up of the syllable denoting Jehovah, and
the word denoting "salvation." In Jesus, the name of
God is *prefixed*, in Isaiah it is *appended*. Jesus therefore
may be rendered, Jehovah—Salvation; *i.e.* Jehovah the
Saviour. Isaiah denotes Salvation—Jehovah; *i. e.* the
Salvation of Jehovah. The same root furnishes one
or two other words which it may be interesting to
notice. Shuah denotes a "cry for help." It is also
used for "wealth." Shevah is another form of it occur-
ing in Psalm v. 2.

"Hearken unto the voice of my *cry*, my King and my God."

Thus "salvation," "riches," and the "cry" of a
suppliant sufferer, are all derived from the same root,
and all find their answer in our Joshua, or Jesus.
His salvation brings not only deliverance for the
captive, but succour to the suppliant, and boundless
riches to the poor. Everything opposed to *bondage*,
straitness, or *oppression;* everything *free*, *ample*,
plenteous, *abundant*, meets and centres in the name,
and person, of the Saviour. Earthly treasures may
enable their possessor to adorn his lordly mansion
with costly pictures, elegant furniture, and all that
may minister to the lust of the eye, and the pride of
life; but it is only by the knowledge of Jesus that
the chambers of the soul can be "furnished with all

precious and pleasant riches." That root Yashah recals to the eye and ear of the reader of the Hebrew Scriptures the thrice-beloved name which is as "ointment poured forth," for the refreshment of the weary heart. It recals the thought of Him who is, to His faithful people,—

> "Their never-failing treasury filled,
> With boundless stores of grace."

Let no one therefore assert that the study of Hebrew roots is a barren and profitless speculation. The rod of Aaron "brought forth buds, and bloomed blossoms, and yielded almonds;" so the radical terms of the Hebrew language, when cultivated with intelligence and care, yield refreshing fruit, pleasant to the spiritual taste, and nourishing to the inner man. Shall the best years of youth be devoted to the pursuit of Greek and Roman learning, and shall nothing be done to advocate the claims, or to expound the beauties of the earliest of all tongues? Shall Homer and Virgil, Demosthenes and Cicero, Thucydides and Livy, be allowed entirely to absorb that mental strength, which might more profitably be expended in seeking a familiar acquaintance with the writings of Moses and the Prophets?

CHAPTER VI.

On the Leading Characteristics of the Hebrew Language.

(*Continued.*)

THE ancient Hebrew, as comprehended within the pages of the Old Testament, is exceedingly limited in its vocabulary. We are not however justified in inferring, that the language, as it existed in the days of David, or Isaiah, was deficient in copiousness. It has, *of all languages generally studied*, the fewest number of vocables; but this fact may be explained simply on the ground that so small a portion of Hebrew authorship has come down to modern times. The number of distinct roots in the ancient Hebrew may be reckoned rather under 2000; and the number of words altogether does not probably exceed 7000 or 8000. It should be observed, however, that on such points, all that we can do is to *approximate* to an exact statement. But, although possessed of so limited a vocabulary, it abounds in synonymous terms, *i.e.*, such terms as express the same generic idea under different aspects. For example, in Hebrew we have, at least, six different words for man :—

(*mǎth* or *měth.*)—A man. Used only in the plural: and in the Ethiopic distinctively applied to a husband, like the word "man," in some provincial dialects of our own country.

(*ǎdǎm.*)—Man—the name of the species—answering to ἄνϑρωπος, in Greek, and *homo*, in Latin. (See Genesis v. 1, 2.)

(*ěnosh*).—Man—frail, weak, mortal.

(*eesh*).—Man—active, energetic, emphatically "a man," like *vir* in Latin, and ἀνηρ in Greek.

(*gever*).—A man, a strong man, a hero.

(*zǎkǎr*).—A man as distinguished from a woman; a male.

Now a very little reflection must serve to convince any one, at all conversant with the nature of language, how much the whole force and meaning of a passage, the energy and point of a sentence, may depend upon the particular one of these six words that the writer may have chosen to employ. Those readers who are capable of consulting the original Hebrew are referred to the following instances in the Book of Job, as illustrative of my meaning:—

Job xi. 3.—Job v. 7; vii. 20; xi. 12; xiv. 1, 10.—Job i. 1, 3, 8; ii. 3.—Job iv. 13, 17; vii. 1, 17; ix. 2; xxv. 6.—The last of which passages may be rendered thus:—

> "How much less mortal man, that is a *reptile!*"
> And the son of Adam, who is a worm!"

Job iii. 3; xiv. 10.—The last of which passages may
be rendered thus :—

> " But the *hero* dies, and is laid prostrate.
> Yea man (every child of Adam) breathes his last, and
> where is he ? "

But it would be impossible within the limits of this
work fully to illustrate the peculiar power of such
synonymes, and the special adaptation of each
particular term to express that very idea it is designed
to convey. There are seven or eight terms for "rain."
Thuş we have "rain in general," "heavy rain,"
"abundant rain," "stormy rain," "hairy, thin, small
rain;" "the former rain," which fell in Palestine
from the middle of October, to the middle of December,
and prepared the soil for the reception of the seed ;
and "the latter rain," which fell in March and April
before the harvest.

Again, there is one word for "sleep," another for
"slumber," and another for "deep sleep," such as that
into which Adam was cast, in order that Eve might be
produced out of his wounded side. There are twelve
terms reducible under the same generic notion of
"seeing;" and seven or eight under that of "speaking."

One term signifies "to look," another "to behold,"
another "to perceive." One, "to look upon with favour;"
another "to glance at," and another "to inspect narrowly
or closely." We have one term for "looking forth as
from a watch-tower," another "to look down from a
height," another "to look upon with envy." We have

one term implying "to speak rashly," another "to speak oracularly," and another "to speak so as to announce, or publish." We have one word for "a lion" in general, another for "a full grown young lion," another for "a lion's cub," and another for "a strong lion." (Psalm xxxiv. 10.) How many passages of the Old Testament might be illustrated by careful reference to the distinctive import of the Hebrew terms which, in these and other instances, the writers have been led to employ!

CHARACTERISTICS OF THE HEBREW LANGUAGE.

(*Continued.*)

IN order more fully to illustrate what has been said relative to the expressive richness of Hebrew, I would direct the attention of my reader to the beautiful phraseology of the xix. Psalm. The literal rendering of the 1st and 2nd verses may be thus given:—

> "The heavens are *telling* the glory of God,
> The firmament *displaying* the work of His hands;
> Day unto day *welleth forth* speech,
> Night unto night *breatheth out* knowledge."

Thus the four distinct terms in the original are preserved in the translation; and the overflowing fullness with which day unto day pours forth divine instruction, and the gentle whisperings of the silent night, are contrasted, as in the Hebrew.

This expressive, self-descriptive quality constitutes the Hebrew, perhaps, the most *picturesque* of all languages. The words do not serve merely to distinguish persons, or objects, but serve, at the same time, to call up before the mind the *qualities* of the objects to which they are applied. A verse of Scripture, read in any faithful translation, will accurately convey the information, or instruction, contained in the original. But the same verse in Hebrew will do more than this. It will suggest to the mind of the intelligent reader a host of interesting associations.

Macaulay remarks of Milton, "The effect of his poetry is produced not so much by what it expresses, as by what it suggests; not so much by the ideas it directly conveys, as by other ideas which are connected with them." The same may be said of Hebrew. *Its terms are suggestive of thoughts, which no version could convey, because pregnant with unuttered meanings which the most faithful translator would fail in attempting to represent in another language.* This fact may serve to show the *kind* of benefit to be derived from the study of the original Scriptures. Such study is not needed, in order that we may rightly understand, and enjoy, the great doctrines of revelation; or, in order that we may apprehend those practical directions, or feel the force of those exhortations which the Scriptures contain. All things needful for life and godliness may be gathered from the prayerful perusal of our common English Bible. But in seeking to feed upon the truth ourselves, or in endeavouring to expound that truth to others, we may be often very much assisted by the suggestive fullness inherent in the terms of the original tongues.

In this particular, the Hebrew is far superior even to the classic languages of Greece and Rome. I am not insensible to the expressive richness and over-flowing copiousness of the Greek. That language has been to me an object of deep interest from early boyhood. Before my revered father thought me old enough to enter upon the study of it, I attempted to learn it *without a teacher.* I well remember, when quite a child, purchasing a well-worn copy of the Greek Testament from one of my play-fellows. It was in a sadly dilapidated condition, and cost me only a few pence; but I looked upon it as a valuable acquisition. When I became a few years older, I set about acquiring Greek, with earnest diligence; and it formed my chief subject of study, during the best years of my early life. It was a pleasant task to me, when emerging out of boyhood, to devote my hours of voluntary solitude to the study of that noble and energetic tongue. "The studious habit that spontaneously seeks retirement," was formed in those early days, and has never been relinquished. During the long college vacation which I spent in the quiet seclusion of the paternal roof, the bright sun, lighting up the surrounding landscape, often invited me to the

E

pleasant fields in vain. Submission to parental
admonition might lead me to seek company or re-
laxation; taste and disposition, combined with a
certain sense of duty, kept me at my books. But, in
those days, I almost entirely neglected the study of
Hebrew. The original of the NEW TESTAMENT was
associated with the poets, orators, and philosophers
of Greece; and I read it with interest. The original
of the OLD TESTAMENT seemed to me harsh, difficult,
and unattractive; and I hardly expected ever to
become acquainted with it. It appeared to me like a
field overgrown with thorns and briars. I knew
nothing of the treasures that were hidden under its
surface.

The above reference to personal history might
seem altogether out of place, were it not a well-
known fact that multitudes of intelligent persons
are labouring under similar prejudices. It was not
until my twenty-third year, that I gave myself, in
good earnest, to the study of the Hebrew. My
acquaintance with it is only that of a learner still.
Judging from the rapidity with which the modern
languages of Continental Europe may be acquired,
persons sometimes entertain most unfounded notions
relative to the amount of time and labour necessary
for the acquisition of an ancient language. I
remember having been once told by a lady, in perfect
simplicity and seriousness, that she understood that a
knowledge of the Hebrew language might be acquired

within the space of six weeks. All such notions originate either from ignorance, or from the impudent assertions of quack teachers. *In six weeks,* some knowledge of the elements may be gained; but, after six years, or even twenty years of study, the successful scholar will find that his very attainments serve to discover to himself how much yet remains to be acquired.

In copiousness of diction, in variety of phraseology, in definite exactness, in capability of indicating distinct shades of meaning, the Greek excels the Hebrew; but in a pervading moral element, and in a species of pictorial expressiveness, the more ancient language bears away the palm. But in order to enjoy this peculiar characteristic, it is not enough that we be able to read the Hebrew Bible grammatically, and so as to translate it into English. We shall fail in appreciating the hidden beauties of the language, except as we trace the words to their radical signi-fication. When read with exactness and intelligence, almost every leading term in a sentence will be found to exhibit traces of its origin, and to picture forth, before the eye, an image of the idea intended to be conveyed.

In the observations I have made, relative to the leading characteristics of the Hebrew language, I have by no means exhausted the subject; but have only thrown out hints which may serve to excite interest and to aid further investigation. I might have endeavoured to illustrate the *sanctity* and *purity, comprehensiveness* and *expressive brevity, sublimity* and *tenderness* by which the original language of the Old Testament is so pre-eminently characterized. But I leave the elucidation of such qualities to the earnest and studious reader.

CHAPTER VII.

On the Advantages Connected with the Study of Hebrew.

HAVING thus briefly exhibited some of the leading *characteristics* of the Hebrew, I would now, in conclusion, advert to some of the *advantages* connected with the study of it.

We are all so constituted by nature, that the exercise of our mental powers is a source of the purest gratification, and the most important self-improvement. The exact study of languages subserves this great object. The Hebrew has claims, simply *as a language*, and still higher claims, as having been constituted the depositary of so large a portion of those truths which God has been pleased to reveal. It may be acquired without the learner having previously attained a knowledge of Greek or Latin, or of any other foreign language. It is not needful that every Christian, or even the majority of Christians, should be acquainted with any other than their mother-tongue; but it is of deep importance, that among Christian scholars, and especially among Christian ministers, there should always be some who are able to read, with intelligence and accuracy, the original language of the Old Testament as well as the New. Even some of our best Commentators have fallen into strange mistakes from trusting to impressions derived from the English translation. Thus, in Genesis xlv. 20, Pharaoh commands Joseph to say to his brethren :—"Regard not your stuff, for the good of all the land of Egypt is yours." On this passage, the excellent Matthew Henry remarks—"What they had in Canaan, he reckoned but *stuff*, in comparison with what he had for them in Egypt ;" and then proceeds to spiritualize this interpretation, "Thus," adds he, "those for whom Christ intends a share in his heavenly glory, ought not to regard the *stuff* of this world ; the best of its enjoyments are but *stuff*, but lumber," &c. Now, the whole of this strain of exposition is founded on an entire mistake. Our translators evidently did not employ the word "*stuff*" in its modern acceptation, as descriptive of that which is, comparatively, of little value. The Hebrew term assuredly conveys no such meaning, but is applied to articles of the most valuable description. As a specimen of the variety of renderings that may sometimes be given to one single word, I may instance some of the many expressions by which this word is represented in the English :—"armour," "bag," "furniture," "instrument," "jewels," "tools," "vessels," "wares," "weapons," &c. The word is applied in such a variety of ways, that, perhaps, no one English term could be found exactly corresponding to it.

And here I would take the opportunity of referring to a mistake into which even educated Christians are apt to fall. Such persons may suppose that the knowledge of *Greek* and *Latin* may afford them *equal* advantages with those attendant upon an acquaintance with the Hebrew. They can, it is true, in doubtful or difficult cases, refer to the Latin Vulgate, or to the Greek Septuagint. Now, let us notice one or two passages, by way of testing the value of such secondary authorities.

In Proverbs xiv. 9, we read in the English version—

> " Fools make a mock at sin ;
> But among the righteous there is favour."

Here there is an apparent want of correspondency between the two members of the sentence. We have recourse for light to the Latin Vulgate, and find the verse rendered thus:—

> " The fool will mock at sin,
> And favour will linger among the righteous."

If we turn to the Septuagint, we find that the translators of that version understood the original very differently, as appears by their rendering of the verse :—

> " The houses of transgressors will need *expiation* ;
> But the houses of the just are acceptable."

This rendering differs considerably from the English
and Latin, but seems to convey a notion contrary to
Evangelical truth. The finding such a translation
may *stimulate* our curiosity, but assuredly cannot
satisfy it ; and the student who seeks for full satisfaction must feel, with all the aid which the venerable
versions of antiquity can render him, still like a person
groping in the dark. Whence did the idea of *expiation*
get into the text of the Septuagint? Why is that
idea entirely wanting in the English translation?
Why is there no trace of it in Jerome's Vulgate? The
reader of the Hebrew Bible has recourse to the original,
and there he finds that the words may literally be
rendered thus :—

> " Fools scoff at the offering for sin ;
> But among the righteous it is an object of delight."

He observes that the word rendered "sin" in the
common versions, is not the term generally so used,
but is the same as that used in the memorable fifty-
third chapter of Isaiah, in verse 10, and rendered
" An offering for sin." Thus interpreted, this proverb
becomes parallel with the declaration of the Apostle,
I. Corinthians, i. 23, 24.

In the instance just noticed, the common translation
is such as to suggest the need of further examination.
Let us take another example, and one in which the
difficulty does not appear to the mere English reader,

but would be suggested by reference to the ancient versions above referred to.

In Proverbs xviii. 8, and xxvi. 22, we find the following sentence :—

> " The words of a talebearer are as *wounds*,
> And they go down into the innermost parts of the belly."

In the Latin Vulgate, we find a two-fold rendering of xviii. 8, either—

> " The words of a double-tongued person are, as it were, simple ;
> Yet these very words penetrate even to the inner parts of the belly."

Or—

> " Fear casts down the sluggard ;
> But the souls of the effeminate shall hunger."

If we turn to xxvi. 22, which ought to be exactly the same, we shall find that the former of these interpretations, very slightly altered, is alone given in the Latin.

On referring to the Septuagint version of xviii. 8, it appears that the second of the Latin interpretations is given by the Greek translators, and xxvi. 22, is thus rendered :—

> " The words of cunning knaves are soft ;
> But they smite even to the inmost parts of the bowels."

Now, amidst all this confusion and variety, one thing is evident. The English rendering, "wounds," was unknown to the authors of the Ancient versions ;

or, at least, those versions afford no support to that
rendering. An intelligent and inquisitive reader
must be greatly perplexed to arrive at the true interpretation of the verse in question. The reader of the
Hebrew—acquainted with the light which modern
philologists have derived from the cognate dialects—
finds that the sense of the proverb, according to the
best authorities, is thus represented :—

" The words of a talebearer (slanderer, calumniator) are as
    delicious viands,
That go down into the innermost parts of the stomach."

Just in the same way as delicious viands gratify the
natural appetite, so the corrupt taste of the depraved
heart is gratified by listening to the tale of scandal.
The term, on which the whole force of the sentence
depends, never occurs elsewhere in the Hebrew
Scriptures. Its derivation and meaning must, therefore, be sought elsewhere, and both of these are
supplied by the Arabic.

Are any disposed to ask—What is the use of such
studies to a Christian ? I ask them in return—What
is the advantage of an exact acquaintance with the
meaning of the Old Testament? If it be granted
that to lose the knowledge of the original languages
of Scripture would be a great and grievous calamity,
then, either the cultivation of such studies must be
given over to the ungodly, or must be taken up by
Christian scholars. Could any intelligent Christian

desire the former alternative? It remains that some of those who have devoted themselves to the ministry of the truth should give themselves to the task of cultivating such studies.

But it may be alleged that this will take them off from more necessary labours. The reply to this is, that whatever takes off ministers in general from their more important duties, it is not, in one case in five hundred, the study of Hebrew. Nay, for a hundred Christian teachers who can read their Greek Testament, you will not find one who has any critical and scholarlike acquaintance with the original language of Moses and the Prophets.

In conclusion, I would remind the reader, that, important as such a subject of study is in itself, any real profit or blessing resulting from it, must depend on the *spirit* and *frame of mind* cultivated by the student. *There is no true satisfaction in anything, apart from its relation to the knowledge and enjoyment of God.* It will profit us nothing to study the Hebrew Bible in an unhumbled, unbelieving, prayerless frame of spirit. If the reader feels led to enter upon this subject of enquiry from motives of curiosity, or from a desire to be admired for superior attainments, I could not advise him to go forward. But, if on the other hand, he should possess a little leisure time, and some measure of capacity for such pursuits; should he, moreover, seek, through the attainment of an acquaintance with the language of the ancient

Scriptures, to understand them better, and to enjoy them more fully, the rectitude of the motive will promote his success. The *written Word* is the appointed *instrumentality*, as the *blessed Spirit* is the revealed *agent* in illuminating our understandings, and graciously impressing our hearts. Every legitimate means of endeavouring to grow in the knowledge of the Word, may be expected to aid us in yielding compliance with the exhortation:—"Grow in grace, and in the knowledge of our Lord and Saviour Jesus Christ."

The great subject of controversy between the Christian church on the one hand, and the various forms of infidelity on the other, is—the Divine origin of the Old and New Testaments. The great subject of controversy between Protestantism and Popery relates to the amount of practical submission due to the authority of *Scriptures acknowledged to be Divine.* But the questions between the several bodies of Protestants relate to the *meaning* of the Word of God. The question among true Protestants is not— Shall Scripture be allowed to decide our differences? but, rather—What deliverance do these Scriptures give? What is the decision they announce? The day is come when ancient traditions, time-honoured observances, venerated creeds, accredited doctrines, must all be upheld or rejected, just in so far as they are found to be in accordance, or otherwise, with the *one* standard from which there is no appeal. At such a time as the present, the minds of Christians are exposed to dangers of the most opposite character. Those whose tempers are ardent and sanguine are in danger of rejecting truth itself, because held by our forefathers, and embodied in ecclesiastical confessions. Those, again, who are differently constituted, are in danger of being so much alarmed at the innovating tendency of others, that they are disposed to reject truth itself, if it come to them under an appearance of novelty. The truly wise man will seek to avoid these opposite dangers. What saith the Scripture? will be his habitual enquiry. And surely, in reference to the Old Testament, a knowledge of the Hebrew language will, instrumentally, assist in ascertaining the reply. A constant reference to God should pervade all our efforts for the acquisition of profitable knowledge. We should cultivate every mental endowment which He hath imparted. We should let no faculty of the mind become torpid for want of exercise— no affection of the heart wither away for want of suitable objects on which it may expend its strength. But, mind and heart should be devoted to Him. Our intellect—our memory—our powers of apprehension and imagination, should be devoted to the habitual perusal and prayerful examination of the lively Oracles; and our tempers and dispositions, our whole cast of character and course of conduct, be moulded and fashioned in accordance with the elevating and purifying principles with which these Oracles are pervaded and imbued.

In carefully studying the writings of Moses and the Prophets, we shall find much to gratify our taste, and to excite our admiration. But it were a melancholy desecration, to allow one's self to stop short at such a result of their perusal. In addition to such a gratification, there should be a constant endeavour after a realization of their sanctifying power. He who so gazes upon that Divine mirror, as to behold the glory of the Lord, and so beholdeth that glory as to be changed into the same image—whether he be skilled in the original, or only able to read his English Bible—attains to that which excelleth all human learning, and has gathered upon his spirit the impress and the earnest of that conformity to Christ in which will consist the essential blessedness of the redeemed. "Whether there be prophecies, they shall fail; whether there be, tongues, they shall cease; whether there be knowledge, it shall vanish away. For we know in part, and we prophecy in part. But when that which is perfect is come, then that which is in part shall be done away." (I. Cor. xiii. 8—10.)

Before concluding this chapter, I think it right to add a few words of an explanatory character, in reference to the subject of improved renderings. In our authorized translation of the Scriptures, there are to be found, both in the Old and New Testaments, many passages which, according to the judgment of all competent scholars, are capable of being more accurately translated. In *many* instances the mistake is so obvious, that an examination of the original suffices to produce entire agreement as to the correction required. But there are not a few passages, about the exact rendering of which, even the most qualified critics are found to differ. Such cases are to be found in all ancient writings. A considerable number occur in the New Testament, and a still larger number in the Old. If there be room for difference of opinion about the correct translation of a passage in a *Greek* writer, much more may we expect such difficulties to occur in the rendering of difficult passages in *Hebrew*. Greek is remarkable for definiteness and perspicuity; Hebrew, on the other hand, from its inherent character as well as from the limited range of its authorship, is far more likely to present difficulties; which are sometimes of such a character, as to leave the meaning, to a certain extent, ambiguous. Such passages are more frequent in Job, the Psalms, and the Proverbs, than in the historical books of the Old Testament. Such being the case, I cannot expect that *every* proposed alteration suggested in this little work will meet with acceptance, even from those to whose judgment I should be disposed to defer. In the rendering I have given of Proverbs xiv. 9, I anticipate that many critics will refuse to acquiesce. That the original is capable of being so translated, without any violence being done to the idiom of the language, I am ready to maintain. But I do not assert that some of the other proposed renderings of the verse may not be capable of being plausibly defended. I am entirely dissatisfied with the rendering given in our English Bible; and I do not know of any modern critic who would be disposed to retain it. Correction is needed, but the most eminent Hebraists differ as to the extent and character of the correction required. I shall be most ready to defer to any qualified critic who will undertake to furnish solid grounds for the rejection of the version I have given, and who will at the same time establish any other rendering on a satisfactory basis.

None but those whose hours of study have been devoted to such enquiries, can estimate the difficulties attending them. Sometimes the leading term in a sentence is one occurring nowhere else within the whole range of the Hebrew Scriptures, so that its meaning must be ascertained either from the kindred dialects, or by the help of the ancient versions. In some instances, our highest authorities differ as to the rendering of such terms. Again, the apparently lax use of the tenses, and the consequent indefiniteness thence resulting, occasions, particularly in Hebrew poetry, considerable obscurity. I confess, that often when grappling with difficulties, and hardly knowing where to look for light—dissatisfied with the dogmatic assertions of the most accomplished critics—I have longed, in reading the Hebrew Bible, for an inspired Greek version; or, as such a desire never can be satisfied, for some association composed of learned and prayerful Christian men, in whom scholarship should be united with reverential regard for the authority of the Divine testimonies. Where learning is altogether wanting, or only of a superficial character, the best of men will always be liable, in difficult cases, to make grievous mistakes. The valuable Commentary of Matthew Henry, and others of a similar class — can never be regarded as of authority in questions of Hebrew scholarship; and, on the other hand, even the profound learning of the most distinguished German critics, being unaccompanied by higher qualifications, fails in many instances to render them trustworthy translators. Why should there be so frequently found a sort of repulsion between men of earnest Christianity and men of high scholarly attainments? Scholarship would be of infinitely more worth if accompanied by prayerfulness; and believing reverence for the Word of God would find most important secondary aid, in the possession of those acquisitions that bear on the exact study of the Divine Oracles.

CHAPTER VIII.

Specimens of Amended Translations from the Old Testament.

GENESIS XLIX.

THE PROPHECY OF JACOB.

1. And Jacob called unto his sons, and said :—
   "Gather yourselves together, that I may tell you
   that which shall befall you in the last days.
2. Gather yourselves together, and hear, ye sons of Jacob:
   And hearken unto Israel your father.
3. Reuben, thou art my first-born,
   My might, and the beginning of my strength,
   Pre-eminent in dignity, and pre-eminent in power :
4. Impetuous as the water-floods, thou shalt not retain
   the pre-eminence,
   Because thou wentest up to thy father's bed :
   Then didst thou defile it :—he went up to my couch !
5. Simeon and Levi are brethren ;
   Their swords are weapons of violence ;
6. O my soul, come not thou into their secret,
   Let not my heart unite in fellowship with them ;
   For in their anger they slew men,
   And in their wantonness they ham-strung oxen.

7. Cursed be their anger, for it was fierce,
And their wrath, for it was cruel.
I will divide them in Jacob,
And scatter them in Israel.

8. Judah, thou art he whom thy brethren shall praise :
Thy hand shall be on the neck of thine enemies :
Thy father's children shall bow down before thee.

9. Judah is a lion's whelp :
From the prey, my son, thou art gone up :
He stooped down, he couched as a lion,
And as a lioness, who shall rouse him up ?

10. The sceptre shall not depart from Judah,
Nor a lawgiver from between his feet,
Until Shiloh come :
And to Him shall the nations yield obedience.

11. Binding his foal unto the vine,
And his ass's colt unto the choice vine,
He washes his garments in wine,
And his clothes in the blood of grapes.

12. His eyes sparkle with wine ;
And his teeth are white with milk.

13. Zebulon dwells by the haven of the sea,
He is a haven for ships,.
His coast stretches to Zidon.

14. Issachar is a strong ass,
Couching down between the cattle-pens.

15. He saw that repose was good,
And the land that it was pleasant,
And he bowed his shoulder to bear,
And became subject to servitude.

16. Dan shall judge his people,
    As one of the tribes of Israel.
17. Dan shall be a serpent by the way,
    An adder in the path,
    That biteth the horse's heels,
    So that the rider falls backwards.
18. For Thy salvation have I waited, O Jehovah !
19. Gad, a troop shall attack him, but he shall drive them
    back at the last.
20. From Asher—rich shall be his food,
    And he shall yield delicacies fit for kings.
21. Napthali—a bounding hind,
    Words of pleasantness he utters.
22. Joseph is a fruitful bough,
    Even a fruitful bough by a well,
    Propelling its branches over the wall.
23. The archers harassed him ; they shot at him ;
    They bitterly persecuted him :
24. But his bow abode in strength,
    And the arms of his hands were made strong,
    By the hands of the Mighty One of Jacob,
    By the name of the Shepherd, the Stone of Israel,
25. By the God of thy Father who will help thee,
    And by the Almighty who will bless thee
    With blessings of heaven above ;
    Blessings of the deep that lieth under ;
    Blessings of the breasts, and of the womb.
26. The blessings of thy Father have prevailed
    Above the blessings of the eternal mountains—
    The glory of the everlasting hills :

May they rest on the head of Joseph,
On the crowned one among his brethren !

27. Benjamin shall ravin as a wolf,
In the morning he shall devour the prey,
And in the evening he shall divide the spoil."

DEUTERONOMY XXXII.

THE SONG OF MOSES.

1. Give ear, O ye heavens, and I will speak ;
And hear, O earth, the words of my mouth.

2. My doctrine shall drop as the rain :
My speech shall distil as the dew :
As the small rain upon the tender herb :
And as the showers upon the grass.

3. Because I will proclaim the name of Jehovah,
Ascribe ye greatness unto our God.

4. He is the Rock—His work is perfect :
For all His ways are judgment,
A God of truth—and without iniquity,
Just and right is He.

5. The crooked and perverse generation have acted
wickedly against Him,
That they are not His children is their disgrace.

6. Do ye thus requite Jehovah,
O foolish people and unwise ?
Is not He thy Father that bought thee ?
Hath He not made thee, and established thee ?

7. Remember the days of old ;
Consider the years of many generations,
Ask thy father and he will shew thee :
. Thine elders and they will tell thee.

8. When the Most High divided to the nations their
inheritance :
When He separated the sons of Adam :
He fixed the boundaries of the peoples,
According to the number of the children of Israel.

9. For the portion of Jehovah is His people ;
And Jacob is the lot of His inheritance.

10. He found him in a desert land :
In a waste, howling wilderness :
He led him about, He instructed him,
He kept him as the apple of His eye.

11. As an eagle stirreth up her nest,
Fluttereth over her young,
Spreadeth abroad her wings, taketh them,
Beareth them on her wings :

12. So Jehovah alone did lead him :
And there was no strange god with him.

13. He made him ride on the high places of the earth,
That he might eat the increase of the fields ;
And He nourished him with honey out of the rock,
And oil out of the flinty rock.

14. Butter of kine, and milk of sheep,
With the fat of well-fed lambs,
And rams of the breed of Bashan, and goats,
With the nourishment of the choicest wheat ;
And thou didst drink the pure blood of the grape.

15. But Jeshurun waxed fat, and kicked,
Thou art waxen fat, thou art overgrown, thou art
covered with fatness.
Then he forsook God his Maker,
And lightly esteemed the Rock of his salvation.

16. They provoked Him to jealousy with strange gods :
With abominations they provoked Him to anger.

17. They sacrificed unto dæmons, not to God,
To gods whom they knew not :
To new gods that came newly up,
Whom your fathers feared not.

18. The Rock that begat thee thou hast abandoned,
And hast forgotten God that formed thee.

19. And when Jehovah saw it He abhorred them,
Because of the provocation from His own sons and
daughters.

20. And He said: "I will hide My face from them :
I will see what their end will be.
For they are a very froward generation :
Children in whom is no faith.

21. They have moved Me to jealousy with that which is
not God :
They have provoked Me to anger with their vanities :
And I will move them to jealousy with those which
are not a people :
I will provoke them to anger with a foolish nation.

22. For a fire is kindled in mine anger,
That shall burn to the lowest hell :
And shall consume the earth with her increase,
And set on fire the foundations of the mountains.

23. I will heap calamities upon them,
 I will spend mine arrows upon them.

24. They shall be emaciated through hunger,
 And consumed with the burning pestilence,
 And with bitter destruction.
 I will also send the teeth of beasts upon them,
 With the hot poison of serpents, [*lit :* the reptiles of
 the dust.]

25. Without, the sword, and within, the terror,
 Shall cut off both the young man and the virgin,
 The suckling and the man of grey hairs.

26. I said : I would scatter them as with the wind,
 I would make the remembrance of them to cease from
 among men,

27. Were it not that I feared the provocation of the enemy:
 Lest their adversaries should not recognize My hand ;
 Lest they should say—'Our hand is high,
 And Jehovah hath not done all this.'

28. For they are a nation void of counsel :
 Neither is there any understanding in them.

29. O that they were wise, that they understood this :
 That they would consider their latter end !

30. How should one chase a thousand :   .
 And two put ten thousand to flight :
 Except their Rock had sold them :
 And Jehovah had delivered them up ?

31. For their rock is not as our Rock :
 Our enemies themselves being judges.

32. For their vine is of the vine of Sodom,
 And of the fields of Gomorrah :

Their grapes are grapes of gall:
Their clusters are bitter.

33. Their wine is the poison of dragons:
And the cruel venom of asps.

34. Is not this laid up in store with me:
And sealed up among my treasures?

35. To me belongs vengeance and recompence,
Their feet shall slide in due time:
For the day of their calamity is at hand:
And the things that are appointed are hastening on."

36. For Jehovah will judge His people,
And repent Himself for His servants,
When He seeth that their power is gone,
And that there is none shut up or left.

37. And He will say—"Where are their gods?
Their rock in which they trusted?

38. Which did eat the fat of their sacrifices:
And drink the wine of their drink-offerings?
Let them rise up and help you,
And be your protection.

39. See now that I, even I, am He,
And there is no God with Me,
I kill, and I make alive:
I wound and I heal:
Neither is there any that can deliver out of My hand.

40. For I lift up My hand to heaven,
And say—' I live for ever.'

41. If I whet My glittering sword,
And Mine hand take hold on judgment,
I will render vengeance to Mine enemies:
And will repay them that hate Me.

42. I will make Mine arrows drunk with blood :
    And My sword shall devour flesh :
    With the blood of the slain and of the captives,
    From the head of the chiefs of the enemies."

43. Rejoice, O ye nations, His people :
    For He will avenge the blood of His servants :
    And will render vengeance to His adversaries :
    And will be merciful to His land and to His people.

DEUTERONOMY XXXIII.

THE BLESSING OF MOSES.

1. Now this is the blessing wherewith Moses,
   the man of God, blessed the children of Israel
   before his death ; and he said :—

2. Jehovah came from Sinai,
   And rose as the sun from Seir unto them ;
   He shined forth from Mount Paran ;
   And came with ten thousands of holy ones ;
   At His right hand was the fire as their guide.

3. Truly he loveth the people,
   All his saints are in thy hand ;
   And they were prostrate at thy feet,
   And received of thy words.

4. Moses commanded us a law :
   Even the inheritance of the congregation of Jacob.

5. And He was king in Jeshurun :
   When the heads of the people were assembled
   Together with the tribes of Israel.

6. Let Reuben live and not die,
   And let not his men be few.

7. And this is the blessing of Judah, and he said :—
   Hear, O Jehovah, the voice of Judah,
   And bring him to his people :
   Let his hands be sufficient for him,
   And be Thou a help against his enemies.

8. And of Levi he said :—
   Let thy Thummim and thy Urim be with thy Holy
     One,
   Whom thou didst prove at Massah,
   And with whom thou didst strive at the waters of
     Meribah.

9. Who said of his father, and of his mother—"I have
     not seen him."
   Neither did he acknowledge his brethren,
   Nor know his own children :
   For they have observed Thy word,
   And kept Thy covenant.

10. They shall teach Jacob Thy judgments,
    And Israel Thy law.
    They shall put incense before Thee,
    And whole burnt sacrifice upon Thine altar.

11. Bless, O Jehovah, his substance,
    And accept the work of his hands :
    Smite through the loins of them that rise against
      him,
    And of them that hate him that they rise not again :

12. And of Benjamin he said :—
The beloved of Jehovah shall dwell in safety by Him :
And Jehovah shall cover him all the day long,
And he shall dwell between His shoulders.

13. And of Joseph he said :—
Blessed of Jehovah be his land :
With the precious gifts of heaven—the dew,
And with the deep springs that lie beneath :

14. And with the precious fruits, the produce of the sun,
And with the precious fruits, the produce of the months;

15. And with the chief things of the ancient mountains,
And with the precious things of the lasting hills,

16. And with the precious things of the earth, and the
fullness thereof.
And let the good will of the Dweller in the Bush
Come upon the head of Joseph,
And upon the crown of the head of him—the crowned
one among his brethren.

17. His glory is like the firstling of his bullock,
And his horns are like the horns of buffaloes.
With them He shall push the people together to the
ends of the earth :
And they are the ten thousands of Ephraim :
And they are the thousands of Manasseh.

18. And of Zebulon he said :—
Rejoice Zebulon in thy going out,
And Issachar in thy tents.

19. They shall call the people to the mountain :
There shall they offer sacrifices of righteousness :
For they shall be satisfied with the abundance of the
seas :

And with treasures hid in the sand.

20. And of Gad he said :—
Blessed be He who enlargeth Gad.
He dwelleth as a lion :
And teareth the arm and the crown of the head.

21. And he saw that the first-fruits were his,
For there, in the portion assigned by the lawgiver, he
    was securely located:
And he went forth, as leading the people,
To execute the justice of Jehovah,
And His judgments with Israel.

22. And of Dan he said :—
Dan is a lion's whelp
He shall leap from Bashan.

23. And of Naphtali he said :—
O, Naphtali, satisfied with favour,
And full of the blessing of Jehovah :
Possess thou the Sea and the South.

24. And of Asher he said :—
Let Asher be blessed in his children ;—
Let him be acceptable to his brethren :
And let him dip his foot in oil.

25. Thy bars shall be iron and brass.
And as thy days, so shall be thy tranquillity.

26. There is none like God, O Jeshurun,
Who rideth upon the heavens, for thy help :
And in His excellency on the sky.

27. The eternal God is thy refuge :
And underneath are the everlasting arms :
He shall thrust out the enemy from before thee :
And shall say—' Destroy them.'

28. Israel then shall dwell in safety alone :
The eye of Jacob shall behold a land of corn and
wine.
His heavens also shall drop down dew.

29. Happy art thou, O Israel, who is like unto thee ?
O people saved by Jehovah !
The shield of thy help.
And who is the sword of thy excellency.
Thine enemies also shall yield thee feigned submission,
And thou shalt tread upon their high places.

II. SAMUEL, XXIII, 1—7.

THE LAST WORDS OF DAVID.

1. Now these are the last words of David :—
The oracle of David, the son of Jesse :
Even the oracle of the man raised up on high :
The anointed of the God of Jacob :
And the sweet psalmist of Israel :

2. The Spirit of Jehovah speaketh by me :
And His word is on my tongue.

3. The God of Israel saith,
To me speaketh the Rock of Israel :
" A righteous one ruleth over men—
Ruleth in the fear of God :

4. And as the light of the morning shall that sun arise
A morning of unclouded brightness,
As the tender grass springing up from the earth after
rain.

5. Shall not my house be thus with God?
For an everlasting covenant hath He made with me—
Ordered in all things and sure.
For will not He promote all my salvation and all my
desire?

6. But the wicked shall be as thorns which must all be
cast out,
For they cannot be taken hold of with the hand,

7. He who would touch them must be full-armed with the
iron and shaft of the spear.
And with fire shall they be utterly burnt in their
dwelling."

Verse 4 has been thus rendered by Dr. Kennicott :—

As the light of the morning ariseth Jehovah ;
A sun, without clouds, for brightness ;
And as the grass from the earth, after rain.

JOB XIX, 23—27.

Job's Prophecy of a Redeemer.

23. Oh! that even now my words were recorded!
Oh! that they were inscribed in a memorial!

24. That with an iron point and lead,
They were graven in the rock for ever!

25. Surely I do know my Redeemer, the Living One ;
And He, the Last, will arise over the dust,

26. And though after my skin this body be consumed,
    Yet in my flesh shall I see God.
27. Whom I shall see for myself, [or " appearing on my
    behalf."]
    And my eyes shall behold Him, and not as a stranger.
    For this my heart languishes within me.

JOB XXVIII.

THE SEARCH AFTER WISDOM.

[In the following chapter there are passages of very great difficulty, about
the exact rendering of which the most eminent critics are not agreed. I
have adopted, with very slight exceptions, the revised version of Dr. Conant.
The 4th and 5th verses are, in the Hebrew, exceedingly obscure. I am not
able to satisfy myself with any of the various suggestions which have been
proposed for the elucidation of their meaning. I wait for further light.]

1. Surely there is a vein for silver,
   And a place for gold which they refine.
2. Iron is taken out of the earth,
   And stone is fused into copper.
3. He puts an end to darkness,
   And searches out to the very end
   Stones of thick darkness and of death shade.
4. He drives a shaft away from man's abode,
   Forgotten of the foot,
   They swing suspended far from men!
5. The earth, out of it goes forth bread;
   And under it is destroyed as with fire.
6. A place of sapphires are its stones,
   And it has clods of gold.

7 The path, no bird of prey has known it;
   Nor the falcon's eye glanced on it;

8. Nor proud beasts trodden it;
   Nor roaring lion passed over it.

9. Against the flinty rock he puts forth his hand;
   He overturns mountains from the base.

10. In the rocks he cleaves out rivers;
    And his eye sees every precious thing.

11. He binds up streams that they drip not;
    And that which is hidden he brings to light.

12. But wisdom, whence shall it be found?
    And where is the place of understanding?

13. Man knows not its price;
    Nor is it found in the land of the living.

14. The deep saith, "It is not with me;"
    And the sea saith, "It is not with me."

15. Choice gold shall not be given in exchange for it;
    Nor shall silver be weighed for its price.

16. It cannot be weighed with gold of Ophir,
    With the precious onyx and sapphire.

17. Gold and glass shall not be compared with it;
    Nor vessels of fine gold be an exchange for it.

18. Corals and crystal shall not be named;
    And the possession of wisdom is more than pearls.

19. The topaz of Ethiopia shall not be compared with it,
    It shall not be weighed with pure gold.

20. Whence then cometh wisdom?
    And where is the place of understanding?

21. Since it is hidden from the eyes of all living,
    And covered from the fowls of heaven.

22. Destruction and death say :—
"With our ears we have heard the fame of it."
23. God understands the way to it,
And He knows the place of it.
24. For He looks to the ends of the earth,
And sees under the whole heaven.
25. To make the weight for the wind,
And He meted out the waters by measure.
26. When He made a decree for the rain,
And a track for the thunder's flash.
27. Then He saw, and He declared it ;
He established it, yea, and searched it out.
29. And unto man He said :—
" Behold the fear of the Lord, that is wisdom ;
And to depart from evil is understanding."

In the above specimens of revised translation, the attentive reader will observe that I have made only a few alterations in the text of our Authorized Version. My object has been, to exhibit illustrations of the importance of comparatively slight corrections. For all practical purposes, I consider that a Revision of our English Bible would be preferable to a new Translation. Ever since the Scriptures were first published in English, the leading Protestant Versions have been successively founded on those which preceded them. To this, the Authorized Version was no exception. It was simply a revised edition of the

Bishop's Bible of 1568, and that again was founded on Cranmer's of 1540. Cranmer's was a revision of Matthews', published in 1537; and this last, which we owe to Rogers, the martyr, was based upon the previous labours of Coverdale and Tyndale. Tyndale's translation of the New Testament, published in 1525 or 1526, together with his labours on the Old Testament, led the way, and furnished the basis, for all the English Translations since published in this country.

Our Authorized Translation probably owes much of its excellence, to the fact of its being the result of frequent and successive revisions. As the Bishop's Bible was a decided improvement on the previous Translation of 1540, so few will be disposed to deny that the former was improved upon by the revisers appointed by King James. But during the 250 years that have elapsed since the last revision was executed— although very great progress, both in England and on the Continent, has been made in those studies connected with biblical interpretation—no further improvement has been attempted. All students of the originals are well aware that many mistakes might be corrected, and some obscure passages set in a clearer light by the labours of judicious and qualified Christian scholars. The substance of the book might be left untouched. The whole cast and character of the style might be left unaffected ; and only such amendments introduced, as would render our English Bible a more exact representation of the Hebrew and Greek Originals. No honest revision would alter a single doctrine ; or affect, in any way, the leading principles of Divine truth. The great saving verities of our holy faith would come out with greater force and clearness. Neither Unitarianism on the one hand, nor Romanism on the other, would gain any advantage from our English Version being more exactly conformed to the original Scriptures.

I proceed now, briefly to notice some of the corrections which I have ventured to make in Genesis xlix. 1—27. The language in verse 4 obviously refers to the crime of which Reuben had been guilty, and which is recorded xxxv. 22. The term rendered *"unstable,"* denotes *"extravagant,"* *"dissolute,"* *"licentious."* It describes Jacob's eldest son, as boiling over with incontinent desires ; and thus, the rendering given in the English version is neither in accordance with the scope of the passage nor with the meaning of the word. Times without number, has the saying been quoted, as illustrating the evils resulting from *instability* of character. When an intelligent reader of his Hebrew Bible hears the passage so quoted by those who have devoted themselves to the ministry of the Word, he can hardly help regretting that such glaring errors should be suffered to remain in a Translation generally so faithful.

The last clause of verse 6 I have corrected in accordance with the reading of the best Hebrew

MSS., and also with the rendering suggested in the margin of our Bibles.

In verse 24 I have ventured to alter the punctuation of one word. The punctuation forms no part of the original text; and, in a case like the present, although I greatly value the Masoretic vowel system, and would protest against the recklessness with which Horsley and Lowth were in the habit of disregarding it, the alteration may, perhaps, be justified by the requirements of the passage. However, I am ready to defer to scholars who may have studied the subject more fully; and may, therefore, have a better title to be heard on such a question. Should any reader demur to the alteration of a single vowel point, let him retain the authorized version of the clause. Few who have at all studied the controversy respecting the vowel system, will uphold the extravagant notions maintained by Buxtorf, Loescher, and others, respecting the antiquity, and consequent authority, of the Masoretic punctuation; but no modern Hebraist would be found disposed to sanction its rejection, or to adopt the absurdities of the school of Parkhurst and his followers. The system is so marvellously self-consistent, so evidently derived from the essential character of the spoken tongue, so universally diffused, so necessary to those who would hold intercourse with the descendants of Abraham, and so valuable, as a help to the student of Hebrew—that only very urgent reasons would induce me, in any instance, to disregard it.

Throughout the prophecy, repeated reference is made to the *signification* of the names of Jacob's sons. It may, therefore, be interesting to the reader, to have before him the exact meaning of each of them. In the following list, the order is in accordance with that adopted by the dying patriarch.

Reuben   = Behold a son.
Simeon   = Hearing with acceptance.
Levi   = Adhesion or union.
Judah   = Praised.
Zebulon   = Dwelling.
Issachar = Hire.
Dan   = Judging.
Gad   = A troop.
Asher   = Happy.
Napthali = My wrestling.
Joseph   = He shall add.
Benjamin = Son of the right hand.

I may just add, that I have thought well to discard the use of italics in the above specimens, from reasons which will be best understood by those who know the difficulties connected with translating from ancient languages. I consider the use of italics by our translators, as originating in their thoroughly upright intentions, and expressive of their scrupulous desire to represent exactly the words of their original. They evidently wished to say neither more nor less than they were warranted in expressing. But this very scrupulosity has sometimes led them into the obscurity of metaphrase. By attempting too literally

to render the *words* of the sacred writers, they have
sometimes failed in conveying their *meaning*. Thus,
in Exodus iii. 6, the language of God to Moses is thus
given in the Authorized Version :

"I *am* the God of thy father," &c.

To this memorable declaration, our Lord refers in
Matthew xxii. 32, and bases his argument on the
mode of expression employed by Jehovah.

Had the verb of existence been in the *past tense*—
had the assertion run thus :—I *was* the God of thy
father, &c.—the inference relative to the undying
existence of the patriarchs would not have been
deducible from the words. The stress is evidently
laid upon the fact, that the verb of existence is in the
present tense. But the English reader finds, on
referring to Exodus iii. 6, that the "*am*" is marked
as an insertion. Why, he may ask, should so much
stress be laid upon what, after all, is not expressed in
the Hebrew original? The answer is obvious to
everyone acquainted with the idiom of the Shemetic
tongues. The *present* tense is necessarily implied in all
such cases by the very structure of the language. The
personal pronoun, if followed by a noun, involves a
proposition, and therefore requires the insertion of
the verb of existence, in order fairly to exhibit the
meaning of the sentence. In such cases, no verb is
used in Hebrew, whereas, had the assertion related
either to the past or the future, we should have found
the verb inserted in the corresponding tense.

Notes on Deuteronomy XXXIII.

In verse 2, I have inserted " as the sun," although there are no corresponding words in the Hebrew. The thought thus expressed is contained in the verb.

As given in our English Version, the passage fails to convey the image suggested to the reader of the original, and to exhibit the connexion between the *early brightness*, expressed by the first verb, and the *noonday splendour*, described by the second.

In verse 14, the idea conveyed in the Hebrew is very obscurely rendered in the Authorized Version. It is difficult to say what our translators understood by " the precious things put forth by the moon." The first clause seems to refer to those crops which are produced annually, and the second clause to those more rapidly growing vegetable productions which the successive months yield for the food of man and beast. The word rendered *moon* in A.V. is plural in Hebrew, and ought to be translated *months*. The cognate term for " moon" is never found in the plural.

The amended rendering of verse 25 is sanctioned by the best authorities ; but the meaning of the term rendered in A.V. " strength" is somewhat doubtful. The rendering of this verse in the LXX. agrees with our Authorized. The Vulgate gives—

" His shoe shall be iron and brass ;
As the days of thy youth, so also shall be thine old age."

II. Samuel XXIII., Verse 1—7.

The brief prophecy entitled "The Last Words of David," is one of the most difficult, as well as one of the most interesting passages recorded in Old Testament history. It may be interesting to give the passage as it stands in the ancient versions, and also as rendered by some of the most eminent of our modern critics. Careful students of Scripture may often derive valuable hints even from those versions, the general character of which is acknowledged to be very defective. In critical accuracy, the more modern versions excel the ancient. But, in spite of these numerous mistakes, the LXX. and Vulgate Versions of the Old Testament often serve to elucidate the meaning of particular terms, and to aid us in the study of the Hebrew Scriptures.

THE LATIN VULGATE,

AS TRANSLATED IN THE DOUAY VERSION.

1. Now these are David's last words. David, the son of
Isai, said: The man to whom it was appointed con-
cerning the Christ of the God of Jacob, the excellent
Psalmist of Israel, said :

2. The Spirit of the Lord hath spoken by me, and His
word by my tongue.

3. The God of Israel said to me, the strong one of Israel
spoke, the ruler of men, the just ruler in the fear of
God.

4. As the light of the morning, when the sun riseth,
shineth in the morning without clouds, and as the grass
springeth out of the earth by rain.

5. Neither is my house so great with God, that He should
make with me an eternal covenant, firm in all things
and assured. For He is all my salvation and all my
will, neither is there ought thereof that springeth
not up.

6. But transgressors shall all of them be plucked up as
thorns, which are not taken away with hands.

7. And if a man will touch them, he must be armed with
iron, and with the staff of a lance; but they shall be
set on fire and burnt to nothing.

THE VERSION OF THE GREEK SEPTUAGINT.

1. AND these are the last words of David: Faithful is David, the Son of Jessæ, and faithful the man whom the Lord raised up to be the anointed of the God of Jacob, and beautiful are the Psalms of Israel.

2. The Spirit of the Lord spoke by me, and His word was upon my tongue.

3. The God of Israel says: A watchman out of Israel spoke to me a parable: I said among men,—How will ye strengthen the fear of the anointed?

4. And in the morning light of God, let the sun arise in the morning, from the light of which the Lord passed on, and, as it were, from the rain of the tender grass upon the earth.

5. For my house is not so with the Mighty One, for He has made an everlasting covenant with me, ready guarded at every time; for all my salvation and all my desire (is) that the wicked should not flourish.

6. All these (are) as a thorn thrust forth, for they shall not be taken with the hand.

7. And a man shall not labour among them; and (one shall have) that which is fully armed with iron and the staff of a spear, and he shall burn them with fire, and they shall be burnt in their shame.

TRANSLATION OF THE ANCIENT SYRIAC VERSION.

1. THESE are the last words of David.
   David, the Son of Jesse, spoke;
   The man who set up the yoke of Christ,
   And of the God of Jacob, said,
   Who uttered the sweet songs of Israel :—
2. The Spirit of the Lord spake in me,
   And His word is on my tongue.
3. The God of Israel said,
   And the Rock of Israel said to me:
   He that ruleth among just men,
   Who ruleth over those that fear God.
4. Like the morning light when the sun ariseth,
   The morning light without clouds.
   Thence from the dawn and from the rain,
   Which maketh the earth to bring forth.
5. Is not my house such with God?
   He hath made with me an everlasting covenant,
   And all things are prepared and secure;
   For He Himself hath accomplished all my pleasure
       and my request.
6. But all the wicked are like rough thorns,
   For none of these are taken with the hand.
7. But when any one is about to take hold of them,
   Then are they burnt with fire utterly.

DR. KENNICOTT'S TRANSLATION.

1. THE oracle of David, the son of Jesse;
   Even the oracle of the man raised up on high:
   The anointed of the God of Jacob;
   And the composer of the psalms of Israel.
2. The Spirit of Jehovah speaketh by me,
   And his word is upon my tongue:
3. Jehovah the God of Israel sayeth;
   To me speaketh the Rock of Israel.

   THE JUST ONE ruleth among men!
   He ruleth by the fear of GOD!
4. As the light of the morning ariseth JEHOVAH;   ˙
   A sun without clouds for brightness;
   And as the grass from the earth after rain.
5. Verily thus is my house with God;
   For an everlasting covenant hath he made with me,
   Ordered in all things, and safely secured:
   For he is all my salvation, and all my desire.
6. But the sons of Belial shall not flourish;
   As a thorn rooted up shall be all of them:
   For they will not be taken kindly by the hand;
7. And the man who shall reprove them,
   Shall be filled with iron and a wooden spear;
   But in the fire shall they be utterly burnt with ignominy.

DR. PYE SMITH'S TRANSLATION.

THESE ARE THE LATER WORDS OF DAVID.

1. THE oracle of David the son of Jessai,
    Even the oracle of the high-raised hero,
    Anointed by the God of Jacob,
    And the delightful author of the songs of Israel.
2. The Spirit of God speaketh by me,
    And His word is upon my tongue;
3. The God of Israel saith,
    To me speaketh the Rock of Israel:
4. Ruling over man is a Righteous One,
    Ruling in the fear of God:
    Even as the light of the morning shall He arise,
    Jehovah, the sun,
    A morning without clouds for brightness,
    (As) after rain the herbage from the earth.
5. Truly thus is my house with God,
    For an everlasting covenant hath He fixed with me,
    Ordered in everything and secured ;
    For (this is) all my salvation and all (my) desire.
6. But the wicked shall not grow.
    As prickles to be moved away, all of them;
    For they cannot be taken with the hand.
7. And the man who shall touch them:
    Will be filled with the iron and shaft of the spear;
    But with fire shall they be utterly burned in their
    dwelling.

MAURER'S TRANSLATION.

1. THESE are the later words of David.
   David the son of Jessai said,
   (Who) was raised up on high,
   The anointed of the God of Jacob,
   And the sweet singer of Israel.
2. The God of Israel spake by me,
   And His word was on my tongue.
3. The God of Israel said
   The Rock of Israel said to me.
4. There shall be a righteous ruler over men,
   A ruler fearing God.
   And (he shall come forth) as the morning light shineth,
   (As) the sun ariseth, (as) the cloudless morning light,
   (As) the grass springeth forth from the earth, by reason
         of the brightness after rain.
5. For shall not my house be thus, with (the help of) God?
   For He hath made with me an everlasting covenant
         ordered in all things, and to be kept,
   For will He not promote all my salvation, and all my
         desire?
6. But the impious shall be all as thorns to be cast out,
   For no one can take them with the hand.
7. He who wishes to take them must be furnished with
         iron, and a spear.
   They shall be burnt with fire in their place.

APPENDIX.

[A. *Page* 11.]

In turning from the study of the pure Hebrew to the so-called Chaldee of Daniel and Ezra, we find, in addition to certain distinct *grammatical* differences, dialectical changes in the *words*. Some of the terms we meet with are the same, both in form and meaning, with those with which we are already familiar. Others again are very slightly altered. A third class are so much disguised, that, at first sight, we are unable to trace their relation to the corresponding terms in the pure Hebrew:—while a fourth class consist of such as are entirely unknown to us, because never found in that form of the language employed by Moses and the Prophets.

Such is the case also with the Aramaic dialect which appears to have been in use during the period in which our Lord and His Apostles were on the earth.

Thus the Hebrew word AB (pronounced AV), becomes, in the dialect then prevalent in Palestine, ABBA. See Mark xiv. 36. Rom. viii. 15. Gal. iv. 6. Here, it will be observed, the alteration consists merely in the addition of a syllable.

H

The Hebrew word for Lord is ADŌN, but in the Aramaic sentence quoted in I. Cor. xvi. 22, we read,

not   ADŌN ATHA,

but   MARAN ATHA—

the Lord cometh.

In the memorable words uttered by the Saviour on the cross, and taken from Psalm xxii. 1, we have a still more important illustration of the differences between the ancient Hebrew and the more modern Dialect.

The Hebrew words, as contained in the Old Testament, may be thus represented in English characters:—

AILEE, AILEE, LAMA AZABTANEE.

While the words, as recorded by the Evangelist, Matt. xxvii. 46, would read thus:—

EELEE, EELEE, LAMA SABACHTHANEE.

Here the difference is altogether slight, except in the last word. The common Hebrew word AZAB, "to forsake," is exchanged for the Aramaic term SABACH. (or rather SHEBACH) which is found in Daniel iv. 12.

It is deserving of notice, that our blessed Lord quoted the words, not in the language in which the Psalm was originally written, but in the Vernacular dialect of the people by whom He was surrounded.

They had therefore no excuse for misapprehending His meaning. Some of them may have understood their application, and afterwards, when the Spirit was poured out from on high, may have savingly experienced their power.

[B. *Page* 12.]

ISAIAH LII. 13—LIII. 12.

AMENDED VERSION.

13. Behold ! my servant shall prosper,
    He shall be raised up, and exalted, and be very high ;
14. Even as many were shocked at Thee,
    (So disfigured was His appearance, more than that of
    man,
    And His form more than that of the sons of men,)
15. So shall He sprinkle many nations ;
    Kings shall shut their mouths because of Him ;
    For what had not been told them, they shall see,
    And what they had not heard, they shall perceive. *

CHAPTER LIII.

1. Who has believed our report,
   And to whom has the arm of Jehovah been revealed ?
2. For He grew up as a sucker before Him, [or them]
   And like a root out of a dry ground,
   He had neither form nor comeliness, that we should
   regard Him,
   Nor beauty, that we should desire Him.
3. He was despised and rejected of men,
   A man of sorrows and acquainted with griefs,
   So that we hid our faces from Him ;
   He was despised and we esteemed Him not.

---

* Or,   For they who had not been told, they see,
         And they who had not heard, they hear.

ISAIAH LII. 13.—LIII. 12.

<small>The Septuagint Version, in English.</small>

13. Behold! My servant shall understand; and be exalted, and glorified exceedingly.
14. As many shall be amazed at Thee, so shall Thy face be inglorious among men; and Thy glory shall not be honoured among the sons of men.

15. Thus shall many nations wonder at Him; and kings shall keep their mouths shut; for they to whom no report was brought concerning Him, shall see; and they who have not heard, shall consider.

CHAPTER LIII.

1. O Lord, who has believed our report,
And to whom has the arm of the Lord been revealed?
2. We brought a report as of a child before Him,
He is as a root in a thirsty land,
He has no form nor comeliness;
And we saw Him, but He had no form or beauty.

3. But His form was ignoble, and inferior to that of the children of men,
He was a man in suffering, and acquainted with the bearing of sickness;
For His face is turned from us,
He was dishonoured, and not esteemed.

4. Yet surely it was our griefs that He bore,
   It was our sorrows that He carried ;
   As for us, we indeed accounted Him stricken,
   Smitten of God and afflicted ;

5. But He was wounded for our transgressions,
   He was bruised for our iniquities ;
   The chastisement of our peace was upon Him,
   And with His stripes we are healed.

6. All we like sheep were gone astray,
   We had turned each to his own way ;
   But Jehovah made the iniquities of us all to fall on Him.

7. He was oppressed and He was afflicted,
   Yet He opened not His mouth.
   As a lamb that is led to the slaughter,
   Or as a sheep before her shearers is dumb,
   So He opened not His mouth.

8. By oppression, and by a judicial sentence, He was
   taken away :
   And who can describe His generation ?
   For He was cut off out of the land of the living :
   For the transgression of my people was He smitten.

9. They had assigned Him His grave with the wicked ;
   But He was with the rich man after His death,
   Because He had done no violence,
   Neither was deceit found in His mouth.

4. He bears our sins, and is pained for us ;
   Yet we accounted Him to be in trouble,
   And in suffering and in affliction.

5. But He was wounded on account of our sins,
   And bruised because of our iniquities ;
   The chastisement of our peace was upon Him,
   And by His bruises we are healed.

6. All we, as sheep, have gone astray ;
   Every one has gone astray in his way ;
   And the Lord gave Him up for our sins.

7. And He, because of His affliction,
   Opens not His mouth ;
   He was led as a sheep to the slaughter ;
   And as a lamb before the shearer is dumb,
   So He opens not His mouth.

8. In His humiliation His judgment was taken away ;
   Who shall declare His generation ?
   For His life is taken away from the earth,
   Because of the iniquities of my people He was led to
   death.

9. And I will give the wicked for His burial,
   And the rich for His death :
   For He practised no iniquity,
   Nor craft with His mouth.

10. But it pleased Jehovah to bruise Him; He put Him to grief.
When His soul shall have made a sacrifice for sin,
He shall see His seed, He shall prolong His days,
And the pleasure of Jehovah shall prosper in His hands.

11. He shall see of the travail of His soul, and shall be satisfied.
By the knowledge of Himself shall He, the Righteous One, my Servant, justify many;
For He shall bear their iniquities.

12. Therefore I will divide Him a portion with the great,
And with the strong He shall divide the spoil;
Because He poured out His soul unto death,
And was numbered with the transgressors,
And bare the sin of many,
And made intercession for the transgressors.

10. The Lord also is pleased to purge Him from His
    stroke,
    If ye can give an offering for sin,
    Your soul shall see a long-lived seed.

11. The Lord also is pleased to take away from Him the
    travail of His soul,
    To show Him light, and to form Him with under-
    standing,
    To justify the just one who serves many well, and He
    shall bear their sins.

12. Therefore He shall inherit many,
    And He shall divide the spoils of the mighty ;
    Because His soul was delivered unto death,
    And He was numbered among the transgressors,
    And He bore the sins of many,
    And was delivered because of their iniquities.

[*C. Page* 22.]

The following are the leading *Principles* on which the System of Schultens is based :—

1. All languages have something *peculiar* and *special ;* something *belonging to them*, both in their derived, and in their primitive meanings, which cannot be transferred to other languages with equal *force, propriety, felicity*, and *fulness.*

2. This characteristic is by far most conspicuous—(on account of the great antiquity of the language)—in the Hebrew, and in its dialects, the Chaldee, the Syriac, and the Arabic.

3. In all languages, each word has only one *primary* and *proper* meaning belonging to it.

4. Yet all languages abound in secondary meanings—as we term them—imparted to them by means of Metaphor, Metonymy, Synechdoche, Irony, Catachresis, and other figures of speech.

5. So great is this copiousness, that the *one radical*, and *proper* force of a single word sometimes spreads out into *thirty, sixty*, a *hundred* or more, *secondary* and *figurative* significations; just as a trunk of a tree will shoot forth principal and smaller branches, in every direction.

6. There is oftentimes not the slightest *resemblance, connexion*, or *agreement*, perceptible between these *secondary* meanings ;—on the contrary, they appear utterly unlike, and even *opposed to one another.* But this can never really be the case in any language properly constructed.

7. It is plainly impossible to discover any mode of reconciling these *contrary,* and *conflicting* significations—at least so as to carry conviction to the mind—unless we have before us the original meaning from which such secondary meanings have been derived.

8. This *original, radical, proper, single* meaning is, in all languages, of very rare occurrence. On the other hand, the *metaphorical,* and other *secondary* meanings, are exceedingly common, and everywhere preponderate.

9. So true and unquestionable is this, that sometimes the *original* force of a word will not once occur in a large book by a copious writer, yea, not even in several books ; while the *secondary* meanings fill every page, and occur times without number.

10. In proportion to the *fewness* of books in any language will be the *difficulty* of investigating the *original* or *radical* ideas from which the *secondary* meanings have been derived.

11. If only *one* work in any language remains which treats copiously and eloquently concerning things human and Divine, it is impossible—from the very nature of language itself—that the *primitive meanings* of the majority of the vocables should be contained in that book; but, as already stated, none of these will appear there, or else they will occur very seldom.

12. Still further, those *radical* meanings, which are not contained in the book itself which we possess, can certainly never be obtained from that source, so as to convince the judgment, even should we spend a whole life in most diligently bringing together, and comparing different places.

13. Those *secondary* ideas, too, which arise by means of metaphors, and other figures of speech, are of so arbitrary a nature, so unconfined and unfettered, that they can never be arrived at, or demonstrated by any human ingenuity, or critical skill, or logical or metaphysical speculation ; but are deducible only from the proper consideration of the *primary* meaning of the term.

14. Inasmuch as these *primary* meanings of Hebrew words cannot be transferred into any vernacular translation, so it is altogether contrary to common sense to endeavour to obtain them from either the ancient or modern versions.

15. Such *primary* meanings as do not .exist in the Hebrew original, still less could have been expressed in the versions.

16. It is plain from the very nature of the thing, and sound reason, that those primary meanings which are not to be found in the book itself, nowhere exist, nor ought to be searched for, except in the *Dialects* of the language, or other *Oriental Tongues.*

17. No *one* of those *Dialects*—amongst which any affinity exists— is sufficient in itself to furnish the primary meanings ; but such investigations require the mutual assistance and light of several of the dialects.

18. It is impossible to arrive at the marrow of a language, and the vivid perception and sense of its *primary* words, by means of lexicons. The continual study of its books and ancient documents, is indispensable for this purpose.*

* Vetus et Regia Via Hebraizandi. Lugduni Batavorum, 1738, p.p. 36—39.

[D. *Page* 25.]

The following sketch of the recent History of Hebrew
Philology, is extracted from a valuable article contributed
to the "Journal of Sacred Literature" several years ago, by
my able and accomplished friend, Rev. F. Bosworth, M.A.,
of Bristol :—

"While Gesenius was thus giving importance to Hebrew
literature, and facilitating its acquisition, the study of the
Indo-European languages had been making rapid advances.
Buttmann, Matthiæ, Thiersch, Zumpt, Bopp, Humboldt,
Rosen, Schlegel, and Grimm, had been striving for higher
aims and more sound results. Grammar was no longer a
mere collection of phenomena, but a science demanding and
deserving philosophical investigation and analysis. The
advancement in classical philology necessarily brought with
it a desire that Oriental literature might share in the benefits
thus largely enjoyed and highly prized. This wish, as far
as Hebrew was concerned, was strengthened by the im-
provements introduced into the study of Arabic, by Rosen,
Kosegarten, and especially De Lacey; and into that of
Ethiopic, by Hupfeld. The honor of having, to any considerable extent, satisfied these new demands, belongs
undoubtedly to Ewald.

"This distinguished scholar was, at the time he published
his 'Critical Grammar of the Hebrew,' Professor in the
University of Gottingen. 'From the appearance of this
work,' says Nordheimer, 'dates the commencement of a new
and important era in Semitic philology.' . . . Basing
his investigations on the philosophical views of language in

general, he has elucidated some of the deepest obscurities of
Hebrew grammar, and raised the study to an equality with
that of the Indo-European tongues.

"Applying the doctrine of sounds to the language, Ewald
has eminently succeeded in giving a life-like character to
this ancient tongue. In treating on the accents, his bold
and keen spirit of research has led to the most valuable
results, and enabled him to show the 'beautiful harmony
between the accentuation and the syntax.' His sections on
'nominal stems,' and 'verbal flexion,' are invaluable; while
his treatment of the syntax is such as scarcely to leave a
difficulty untouched. . . . . .

"While Ewald, the uncompromising and sometimes
bitter opponent of Gesenius, was thus prosecuting his
researches, and publishing his works, Hupfeld, a pupil, and
subsequently the successor of the great Halle Hebraist, was
preparing a new Hebrew grammar, 'which,' says Tholuck,
'must surpass that of Ewald in the fundamental character
of its researches.' As early as 1825, three years before
Ewald's first Grammar was published, Hupfeld printed his
first work 'Exercitationes Ethiopicæ,' in which he presented
to the world his researches into the doctrine of sounds, and
well illustrated the quadriliteral and quinquiliteral forms in
Hebrew, from Ethiopic sources. His views were more fully
carried out, and much light thrown upon the language, by two
subsequent Essays. Indeed, all the writings of this eminent
scholar are of the greatest value to the student of Hebrew—
distinguished as they are by profound erudition, no less
than by a careful avoidance of extreme views. . . . .

"Shortly after the publication of Ewald's Critical
Grammar, the increasing attention paid to Philology led to

so successful a comparison of languages, as to call for the formation of a new science—that of Comparative Philology. Bopp, Pott, and W. de Humboldt, were the great leaders of the movement. The connexion between the so-called Semitic tongues had been, at least to some extent, long known ; and valuable aid in the study of Hebrew had been afforded by means of the cognate dialects. The union between the Indo-Germanic languages was a discovery of later years. It could not but be, that the impulse given to the study of these two families of languages, should lead to the desire to inquire into their relationship. The result was, that the Semitic family was no longer found to occupy an isolated position, but was connected with the other great families of tongues, and, with them, forms the great object of Comparative Philology. It was beginning to be felt, that the true solution of the contrast of stability and fluctuation which is found in language, lies in the unity of human nature. The question, however, still remained, and is not answered yet—What is the connexion between the Semitic and Indo-Germanic families ?

"Gesenius, who in his Latin Manual, in 1833, was the first to deduce lexical analogies from the Indo-Germanic tongues, asserted at the same time, that the connexion between the languages was but remote. Roediger, the pupil of Gesenius, and the editor of his Grammar, is still more decided. He says, that though a remote relationship exists between these families, which renders comparison valuable for lexicography ; they 'do not stand in a sisterly, or any close relationship to each other.'

" Other scholars have been induced to think differently. In 1834, Lepsius traced some striking resemblances between the Hebrew and the Sanscrit; and the year after, in letters to Chevalier Bunsen, proved the remarkable agreement between the numerals in Coptic, Semitic, and Indo-Germanic; and announced, that his discovery of the meaning of the ancient numeral roots, had placed the whole cycle of Semitic and Indo-Germanic languages 'in a very remarkable harmony with one another.' Three years later, Nordheimer, in the preface to his excellent Hebrew grammar, affirmed it to be one of the objects he had in view, in treating of the Hebrew language, ' to point out its surprisingly intimate connexion, both lexicographical and grammatical, not only with the other Semitic languages, but also with those of the Japhetish or Indo-European stock.'

" This object was still more steadily pursued by Furst, who may be said to have founded the third school of Hebrew study. He, Delitzsch, Caspari, and others, while they style the school of Gesenius, the *empiric*, and that of Ewald, the *rational*, term their own, the *historico-analytic*: making, as they do, equal use of the writings of the Rabbins, the philosophy of speech, and the comparison of languages. Cultivating with the utmost assiduity and success Talmudic learning, they at the same time, boldly, and sometimes rashly, as it appears to us, make the greatest use of the Sanscrit, claiming for it a close and sisterly relation to the Hebrew.

" Furst boldly asserts, that of the list of 375 Sanscrit roots given by Pott, whose meaning is established beyond a doubt, there is not one which is not also Semitic. In defence of the same views, Delitzsch wrote his 'Jesurun.' It was reserved for Meier, however, to theorize most daringly in this direction. In his large work, 'Hebräisches Wurzelwörterbuck,' 1845, he asserts, that the simplest form of the verb in Hebrew, in the perfect, has been formed from monosyllabic roots, by the *reduplication of the radical syllable,* just as in Sanscrit, Gothic, Greek, and Latin. . .

"It is worthy of remark, that while an almost exclusive reference to tradition distinguished the first students of Hebrew, and a peculiar fondness for the use of the cognate dialects marked the scholars of the Reformation, and the early Dutch philologians, all the sources of information are now open, and are, alike and in union, brought to bear upon the study in question. Thus, while Ewald and his followers are, with the greatest success, pursuing the philosophical study of Hebrew; and while Winer, Hupfeld, Bernstein, and Roediger, are displaying the riches of the cognate dialects ; Zunz, Sachs, and others, are placing their researches in ancient Hebrew literature within the reach of students ; and Furst, Delitzsch, and Lassen are throwing light upon the ancient Scriptures from the sacred tongue of the Hindoos. Especially active at present, are the Hebrew scholars in Germany, in the direction of comparative philology and the early literature of the language." *

* See Journal of Sacred Literature, Jan. 1853, pp. 429—436.

ON THE HEBREW POINTS.

MANY of my readers, although unacquainted with the
Hebrew language, may probably have heard of the
controversy respecting the Vowel Points. According to
the system adopted by the Jews themselves, and by almost
all Christian scholars, the twenty-two letters of the
Hebrew Alphabet are all reckoned as consonants. There
is very strong reason for believing that, so long as the
Hebrew continued to be a spoken language, the vowels
were generally left to be supplied by the reader from his
previous familiarity with the words. Thus, to any one
familiar with English, such a sentence as the following
would occasion no difficulty:—

"Blck brds bld nsts."

If *a* were denoted by – and *i* by . and *ui* by : and *e* by '
the words might be written more fully thus:—

"Blck brds bld nsts,"
   –   .   :   '

so that the dullest reader might be able to pronounce them.
This simple illustration may serve to explain the use of
the marks employed in Hebrew to designate the vowel-
sounds. As long as Hebrew was a living language, such
marks were scarcely at all needed. In the sixth or seventh
centuries of the Christian era the system of marks for the
vowels was invented, evidently with the view of perpetuating
the mode of pronunciation which the Jews had received
from their forefathers.

The controversy respecting the antiquity, and consequent authority, of the points, might have been much more easily settled, had the learned disputants only been led to define with exactness the terms of the question. There is no reasonable ground for maintaining that the *marks* and *names*, by which the vowels are now expressed, were in use when the Hebrew Scriptures were written; but, on the other hand, it is quite certain that the *system of vowel-sounds*, or something analogous, was in use centuries before the *marks* were appended to indicate the pronunciation; just as the words of our own language were pronounced in accordance with certain rules, before any pronouncing dictionary had been given to the world. Just as, in certain systems of Stenography, the vowels are, for the most part, left to be supplied by the reader, so the Hebrew language was originally written without the marks that indicate the correct vocalisation. Words consisting of the same letters were differently sounded according to their difference of meaning; but the meaning was left to be gathered from the context, and the obvious meaning guided the mode of pronunciation. Thus DBR, if intended to denote "pestilence," was sounded DeBeR; but, when used to signify "a word," it was pronounced DaBaR. This instance is expressly given by Jerome, in his Commentary on Habakkuk iii. 5. This most learned of all the fathers of the Church was evidently acquainted with the *vowel-sounds*, but makes no reference to the *marks* by which those sounds were afterwards indicated. The former were inherent in the living language : the latter were invented at a later period, to preserve distinctions which might otherwise have been lost. Surely much precious time might have been saved, and much unseemly controversy been prevented, had the above explanation of the matter been accepted by the eminent scholars of the sixteenth century, who advocated extreme and untenable opinions on both sides of the question at issue.

. If Buxtorf and his followers were influenced by prejudice, in defending the antiquity of the whole system, Capellus and his disciples were, at least, equally mistaken in their rejection of so venerable a guide to the correct pronunciation of the ancient Hebrew. When, about thirty-five years ago, I began the study of Oriental learning at the University of St. Andrews, the system there pursued was founded on the views of Capellus, and in accordance with the mode re-commended by the laborious but fanciful Parkhurst. On taking up the study with more earnestness, some years afterwards, I found that the anti-punctist system was generally discarded by Hebrew scholars, both in England and on the Continent. Increased familiarity with the language has only served to strengthen my conviction of the value of the vowel-system, as incomparably the most reliable guide to the ancient pronunciation. The system adopted by Parkhurst, appears to me, entirely without foundation; and no language would be too strong to express my sense of its absurdity. If some learned foreigner should assert, that because he had found the words "Brd nd chs fr sppr" written in short-hand without the vowels for the sake of brevity, therefore, the proper pronunciation of the words was to be so represented, he would hardly be guilty of a greater error than that into which those who reject the vowel points have fallen.

Berd for *bread*, *ches* for *cheese*, *fer* instead of *for*, *sepper* instead of *supper*, sound no more strange to the ear of an Englishman, than the anti-punctist mode of reading Hebrew sounds in the ear of a Jew acquainted with the language of his own Scriptures. The above observations may, perhaps, serve in some measure to satisfy the laudable curiosity of those readers who have heard something respecting the two different modes of pronouncing Hebrew words, but may have felt a wish for further information respecting the subject. If anyone would wish to go deeply into the question, let him, by all means, consult a most elaborate and valuable treatise, entitled "Hebrew in the time of Jerome," inserted in the sixth number of the "Journal of Sacred Literature" (First Series), by my friend, Mr. Bosworth, the learned and laborious Pastor of the Church meeting in King Street Chapel, Bristol. Amidst the general neglect of Hebrew learning, by those who have devoted themselves to pastoral labours, I am thankful that some of those so occupied, in our own city, have given themselves to the study of their Hebrew Bible. The article to which I have just referred must have required many months of studious investigation before it could have been written, and deserves to be better known, and more extensively circulated.

I do not know that I can more profitably sum up all that I should wish to add, respecting the subject of these concluding observations, than by laying before the reader the following extract from an article by Dr. John Nicholson, which occurs under the word "Hebrew," in Kitto's "Cyclopædia of Biblical Literature."

" The origin of the vowel-points is to be ascribed to the effort which the Jewish learned men made to preserve the pronunciation of their sacred language at a time when its extinction, as a living tongue, endangered the loss of the traditional memory of its sound. Every kind of evidence renders it probable, that these signs for the pronunciation were first introduced about the seventh century of the Christian era, that is, after the completion of the Talmud ; and that the minute and complex system which we possess, was gradually developed, from a few indispensable signs, to its present elaborateness. The existence of the present complete system can, however, be traced back to the eleventh century. The skilful investigation of Hupfeld (in the Studien und Kritiken of 1830), has proved that the vowel-points were unknown to Jerome and the Talmud ; but, as far as regards the former, we are able to make a high estimate of the degree to which the traditionary pronunci- ation, prior to the use of the points, accorded with our Masoretic signs : for Jerome describes a pronunciation, which agrees wonderfully well with our vocalisation. We are thus called on to avail ourselves thankfully of the Masoretic punctuation, on the double ground, that it represents the Jewish traditional pronunciation, and that the Hebrew language, unless when read according to its laws, does not enter into its full dialectual harmony with its Syro-Arabian sisters."

I have thought it well to append to this little work on the Hebrew Language, a paper in relation to a question which has recently been agitated in connexion with the circulation of the Holy Scriptures.

OUGHT PROTESTANT CHRISTIANS TO AID IN THE CIRCULATION OF ROMAN CATHOLIC TRANSLATIONS OF HOLY SCRIPTURE?

The recent Discussions, relative to the Circulation of Roman Catholic Translations of the Bible on the Continent of Europe, have necessarily excited considerable interest among all who truly appreciate the value of Holy Scripture. Very decided judgments have been arrived at, by Christian men, on both sides of the question. Many consistent Protestants, who cannot at all be suspected of the slightest leaning towards Romanism, are inclined to uphold and advocate the course hitherto pursued by the Bible Society, whose agents endeavour to reach the hearts and consciences of ignorant Roman Catholics through means of such Translations as are approved and sanctioned by their own Church; while other upright and zealous Christians condemn such a course as almost equivalent to acting on the principle of doing evil that good may come out of it.

There is evidently, among the generality of good men, a readiness to adopt decided opinions, on such subjects, without taking the pains to furnish themselves with the information on which all legitimate judgments must be based. Patient enquiry should ever precede positive convictions. On the whole subject of the Ancient Version

denominated the Vulgate—the only authentic and standard
Bible in the Church of Rome, and the source whence the
Translations above referred to have been derived—an
incredible amount of ignorance and misapprehension pre-
vails, even among intelligent Christians.

In such a state of things, it has appeared to me that aid
might be obtained towards settling the matters in dispute,
were certain leading facts, relative to the Vulgate, put forth
in such a way as to be within the reach of general readers
interested in the deeply important question of Bible
circulation. There is no work in the English language, so
far as I am aware, wherein the subject is treated in a
manner at once scholarly and yet popular, condensed and
yet clear, comprehensive and yet free from overmuch
critical minuteness. As a step towards supplying this
desideratum, and with the view of bringing the subject
before the notice of those Christian scholars whose studies
and tastes may dispose them to such an undertaking, I have
drawn up the accompanying Prospectus. Very few English
scholars would be qualified to fill up the sketch here
presented, without being indebted to the help of those who
may have made one or other of the matters involved in the
execution of the plan here proposed the subject of their
more special attention. But if some few of our more
advanced Biblical scholars were to take up the idea and
improve upon it, the result might tend to furnish to
intelligent Christians at large a very considerable amount
of most interesting information bearing on practical
questions connected with the circulation of Roman Catholic
versions in any part of Christendom.

PROSPECTUS OF A MONOGRAPH ON THE VULGATE.

APPENDIX.

ON THE REVISION

OF OUR

ENGLISH BIBLE.

ON THE REVISION

OF OUR

ENGLISH BIBLE.

ALL intelligent Christians in England must feel a greater or less degree of interest in the subject of the following pages. No one can truly understand the importance of the question at issue, without desiring to form a correct judgment respecting it. Yet there are many who seem to take little or no interest in the matter, and there are not a few others whose opinions appear to have been formed without any careful enquiry into the facts of the case, or any thoughtful consideration of the reasons that may be urged on both sides of the question at issue. The far larger number of those who reverence and prize their Bibles are so ill-informed respecting the grounds on which a revision is considered desirable, that they are not, at present, in a position to give any opinion which ought to weigh with others; while often those who are the least instructed, are, at the

same time, the most obstinately attached to the
sentiments which they have been led to adopt.

In regard to matters of a worldly nature, people
generally consider themselves bound to *examine*,
before they *decide;* but, while not one out of a
thousand Christians is capable of judging of the
perfect accuracy claimed by some for our common
Translation, hundreds are ready to oppose the idea
of its being capable of improvement. There are
only two classes of Christians, it seems to me, whose
judgment on such a question can be deemed of any
real value; the class who have studied the original
Scriptures for themselves; and the still larger class,
who, though not in a position to judge from their
own personal investigation, are yet well-informed
respecting the sentiments of those who, from the
whole course of their studies, and their Christian
character, have a right to be heard in reference to the
expediency or necessity of revising the Translation
which has been so long in use amongst us. The
decision of the question cannot be left entirely in
the hands of Christian scholars; the vast body of
upright and consistent Christians, who may not be
acquainted either with Greek or Hebrew, ought to
be deferred to, in a matter so important to their
spiritual interests; but the judgments of this larger
class, must, to a great extent, be directed and guided
by the information derived from the studious investigations of the few who have made the Original

Scriptures, in whole or in part, the subject of their habitual study. I say, in whole or in part, for there are many who have a right to be heard in reference to the Translation of the New Testament, who, being ignorant of Hebrew, can only judge at second-hand respecting the accuracy of our Version of the Old Testament.

Previously, then, to any direct steps being taken in so important and deeply responsible a movement as that to which the above remarks have reference, the diffusion of sounder views and larger information on the whole subject must be earnestly aimed at. The Christian mind of England must be enlightened. Prejudices, which are the natural progeny of ignorance, must be patiently met, and courteously removed. Christian scholars must seek to follow the example of Ezra, as recorded in the 8th chapter of Nehemiah, and endeavour to impart to the people the sense of the matter—the right understanding of the whole subject of Biblical Translation.

To this object the following pages are devoted, and, as preparatory to my own remarks, I judge it well to lay before the reader the truly moderate, judicious, and scholarly observations of two of the most distinguished of those who have given to the Christian Church the benefit of their judgment on this great question.

"It is clear that the question—Are we, or are we not, to have a new translation of Scripture? or rather,—since few would propose this, who did not wish to lift anchor and loosen from its moorings the whole religious life of the English people,—Shall we, or shall we not, have a new revision of the Authorized Version?—is one which is presenting itself more and more familiarly to the minds of men. This, indeed, is not by any means the first time that this question has been earnestly discussed; but that which distinguishes the present agitation of the matter from preceding ones is, that on all former occasions the subject was only debated among scholars and divines, and awoke no interest in circles beyond them. The present is apparently the first occasion on which it has taken serious hold of the popular mind. But now indications of the interest which it is awakening reach us from every side. America is sending us the instalments—it must be owned not very encouraging ones—of a New Version, as fast as she can. The wish for a revision has, for a considerable time, been working among Dissenters here; by the voice of one of these it has lately made itself heard in Parliament, and by the mouth of a Margaret Professor of Divinity in Convocation. Our Reviews, and not only those which are specially dedicated to religious subjects, begin to deal with the question of revision. There are, or a little while since there were, frequent letters in the newspapers, either urging such a step, or remonstrating against it; few of them, it is true, of much value or weight; yet at the same time showing how many minds are now occupied with the subject.

"It is manifestly a question of such immense importance, the issues depending on a right solution of it are so vast and solemn, that it may well claim a temperate and wise discussion. Nothing is gained on the one hand, by vague and general charges of inaccuracy brought against our version; they require to be supported by detailed proofs. Nothing on the other hand is gained, by charges and insinuations against those who urge a revision, as though they desired to undermine the foundations of the religious life and faith of England; were Socinians in disguise, or Papists—Socinians, who hoped that in another translation, the witness to the divinity of the Son and of the Spirit might prove less clear than in the present—Papists who desired that the authority of the English Scripture, the only Scripture accessible to the great body of the people, might be so shaken and rendered so doubtful, that men would be driven to their Church, and to its authority, as the only authority that remained. As little is the matter profited, or in any way brought nearer to a settlement, by sentimental appeals to the fact that this, which it is now proposed to alter, has been the Scripture of our childhood, in which we and so many generations before us first received the tidings of everlasting life. All this, well as it may deserve to be considered, yet, as argument at all deciding the question, will sooner or later have to be cleared away; and the facts of the case, apart from cries, and insinuations, and suggestions of evil motives, and appeals to the religious passions and prejudices of the day, apart, too, from feelings which in themselves demand the highest respect, will have to be dealt with in that spirit of seriousness and earnestness which a question affecting so profoundly the whole moral and spiritual life of the

K

English people, not to speak of nations which are yet unborn, abundantly deserves.

"It is no main and leading purpose in the pages which follow, either to advocate a revision, or to dissuade one; but rather I have proposed to myself to consider the actual worth of our present translation; its strength, and also any weaknesses which may affect that strength; its beauty, and also the blemishes which impair that beauty in part; the grounds on which a new revision of it may be demanded; the inconveniences, difficulties, the dangers it may be, which would attend such a revision; some of the rules and principles, according to which it would need, if undertaken at all, to be carried out; and thus, so far as this lies in my power, to assist others, who may not have been able to give special attention to this subject, to form a decision for themselves. I will not, in so doing, pretend that my own mind is entirely in equilibrium on the subject. On the whole, I am persuaded that a revision ought to come; I am convinced that it will come. Not, however, let us trust, as yet; for we are not as yet in any respect prepared for it; the Greek (I mean that special Hellenistic Greek here required), this, and the English no less, which would be needful to bring this work to a successful end, might, it is to be feared, be wanting alike. There is much of crude and immature in nearly all the contributions which have been, and for some time yet will be made, to this object. Nor, certainly, do I underrate the other difficulties which would beset such an enterprise; they look, some of them, the more serious to me the more I contemplate them. Still, believing that this mountain of difficulty will have to be surmounted, I can only trust and confidently hope, that it, like so many other mountains, will not on nearer approach, prove so formidable as at a distance it appears. Only let the Church, when the due time shall arrive, address herself to this work with earnest prayer for the Divine guidance, her conscience bearing her witness, that in no spirit of idle innovation,—that only out of dear love to her Lord and His truth, and out of an allegiance to that truth which overbears every other consideration, with an earnest longing to present His Word, whereof she is the guardian, in all its sincerity to her children,—she has undertaken this hard and most perilous task, and in some way or other, every difficulty will be overcome. Whatever pains and anxieties the work may cost her, she will feel herself abundantly rewarded, if only she is able to offer God's Word to her children, not, indeed, free from all marks of human infirmity clinging to its outward form,—for we shall have God's treasure in earthern vessels still,—but with some of those blemishes she knows of removed, and altogether approaching nearer to that which she desires to see it; namely, a work without spot, or wrinkle, or any such thing; a perfect copy of an archetype that is perfect!

"In the meantime, while the matter is still in suspense and debate, while it occupies, as it needs must, the anxious thoughts of many, it cannot misbecome those who have been specially led by their duties or their inclinations, to a more close comparison of the English Version with the original Greek, to offer whatever they have to offer, be that little or much, for the helping of others towards a just and dispassionate judgment, and one founded upon evidence, in regard to the question at issue. And if they consider that a revision ought to come, or, whether desirable or not, that it will come, they must wish to throw in any contribution which they have to make toward the better accomplishing of this object. Assuming that they have any right to mingle in the controversy at all, they may reasonably hope, that even if much which they bring, · has long ago been brought forward by others, or must be set aside from one cause or another, yet that something will remain, and will survive that rigorous proof to which every suggestion of change should be submitted. And in a matter of such high concernment as this, the least is much. To have cast in even a mite into this treasury of the Lord, to have brought one smallest stone which it is permitted to build into the walls of His house, to have detected one smallest blemish that would not otherwise have been removed, to have made, in any way whatever, a single suggestion of lasting value, towards the end here in view, is something for which to be for ever thankful." (On the Authorized Version of the New Testament, &c., by Richard Chevenix Trench, D.D., Dean of Westminster. Parker, London, 1859, p.p. 1—6.)

"What is the present state of feeling with regard to a revising of our present Version? It seems clear that there are now *three* parties among us. The first, those who, either from what seem seriously mistaken views of a Translation of the Holy Scripture, or from sectarian prejudice, are agitating for a *new* Translation. The second, those who are desirous for a revision of the existing

Version, but who somewhat differ in respect of the proposed alterations and the principles on which they are to be introduced. The third, those who from fear of unsettling the religious belief of weaker brethren are opposed to alterations of *any* kind ; positive and demonstrable error in the representation of the words of Inspiration being, in their judgment, less pernicious than change. Of these three parties, the first is far the smallest in point of numbers, but the most persistent in activities : the second class is daily increasing, yet at present greatly inferior both in numbers and influence to the third.

"Which of these three parties will prevail? We may fervently trust not the first. Independently of the extreme danger of unsettling the cherished convictions of thousands, of changing language that has spoken to doubting or suffering hearts, with accents that have been to them like the voice of God Himself,—independently of reversing a traditional principle of revision that has gained strength and reception since the days of Tyndale,—independently of sowing a strife in the Church, of which our children, and children's children may reap the bitter fruits,—independently of all these momentous considerations,—have we any good reason for thinking that, in a mere literary point of view, it would be likely to be an improvement on the Old Translation? The almost pitiable attempts that have appeared in the last twenty years, under the name of New Translations, the somewhat low state of Biblical scholarship, the diminishing and diminished vigour of the popular language of our day, are facts well calculated to sober our expectations, and qualify our self-confidence.

" But are we unreservedly to join the third party? God forbid. If we are truly and heartily persuaded, that there are errors and inaccuracies in our Version, if we know that though by far the best and most faithful translation that the world has ever seen, it still shares the imperfections that belong to every human work, however noble and exalted, if we feel and know that these imperfections are no less patent than remediable, then surely it is our duty to Him who gave that blessed Word for the guidance of man, through evil report and through good report, to labour by gentle counsels to supply what is lacking, and correct what is amiss, to render what has been blessed with great measures of perfection, yet more perfect, and to hand it down thus marked with our reverential love and solicitude, as the best and most blessed heritage we have to leave to them who shall follow us.

" It is in vain to cheat our own souls with the thought that these errors are either insignificant or imaginary. There *are* errors, there *are* inaccuracies, there *are* misconceptions, there *are* obscurities, not indeed so .many in number, or so grave in character, as the forward spirits of our day would persuade us of,—but there *are* misrepresentations of the language of the Holy Ghost, and that man, who, after being in any degree satisfied of this, permits himself to lean to the counsels of a timid or popular obstructiveness, or who, intellectually unable to test the truth of these allegations, nevertheless permits himself to denounce or deny them, will, if they be true, most surely at the dread day of final account, have to sustain the tremendous charge of having dealt deceitfully with the inviolable Word of God.

"But are we to take no thought of the weaker brethren whose feelings may be lacerated, or whose conscience may be offended by seeming innovations? That be far from us. We must win them by gentle wisdom, we must work conviction in their minds by showing how little, comparatively speaking, there is that is absolutely wrong,—how persuasively it may be amended,—how we may often recur to the expressions of our older Versions, and from those rich stores of language, those treasures of pure and powerful English, may find the very rectification we would fain adopt, the very translation we are seeking to embody in words. No revision of our Authorized Version, can hope to meet with approval or recognition, that ignores the labours of those wise and venerable men, who first enabled our forefathers to read in their own tongue of the marvellous works, and the manifold wisdom of God.

"Let there be, then, no false fears about a loving and filial revision of our present Version. If done in the spirit, and with the circumspection that marked the revision of that predecessor to which it owes its own origin and existence, no conscience, however tender, either will or ought to be wounded. Nay, there seems intimation in their very preface, that our last translators expected that others would do to them as they had done to those who had gone before them; and if they could now rise from their graves and aid us by their counsels, which side would they take? Would they stay our hands if they saw us seeking to perfect their work? Would they not rather join with us, even if it led sometimes to the removal or dereliction of the monuments of their own labour, in laying out yet more straightly the way of divine Truth?

" How this great work is to be accomplished in detail is not for such a one as me to attempt to define. This only I will say, that it is my honest conviction that for any *authoritative* revision we are not yet mature, either in Biblical learning or Hellenistic scholarship. There is good scholarship in this country, superior probably to that of any nation in the world, but it has certainly not yet been sufficiently directed to the study of the New Testament (for of the New Testament only am I now speaking), to render any national attempt at a revision either hopeful or lastingly profitable. Our best and wisest course seems to be this— to encourage small bands of scholars to make independent efforts on separate books, to invite them manfully to face and court impartial criticism, and so by their very failure, to learn practical wisdom, and out of their censors to secure coadjutors, and by their partial successes to win over the prejudiced and the gainsaying. If a few such attempts were to be made and they were to meet with encouragement and sympathy, such a stimulus would be given to Biblical studies that a very few years would elapse before England might be provided with a company of wise and cunning craftsmen into whose hands she might hopefully confide her jewel of most precious price." (A Critical and Grammatical Commentary on the Pastoral Epistles, by Rev. C. J. Ellicott, M.A., Preface, pp. xi.—xv.)

Having thus sought to secure the attention of the reader to the following suggestions, I proceed to state some of the grounds on which I am ready to maintain the expediency of revising our English Translation of the Scriptures.

1. I undertake to prove, before any jury of qualified scholars, that, while our English Version is, probably, the very best of all modern Translations, yet there are to be found in it hundreds of passages in which the sense of the Original is rendered *obscurely*, or *unintelligibly*, or *in which the meaning is entirely misrepresented.* I maintain that by a careful revision, many passages which are, to mere English readers, obscure, would become plain; others which convey no meaning, would be rendered in intelligible language; and many which at present convey a wrong impression of the sense, would be found to express the meaning with accuracy and clearness.

2. That no intelligent reader of the Hebrew and Greek Scriptures can attempt, honestly and fully, to expound the meaning of the Scriptures in public, without being under the necessity of frequently correcting our Translation, in order more accurately to bring out the sense, and that, therefore, it is requisite that some effort should be made to furnish the readers of our English Bible with suitable helps towards the correction of passages which are incorrectly rendered.

3. That the question relative to the matter at issue ought not to be looked at, or decided, under the influence of feeling or predilection, but, like all similar questions, must be determined according to

the facts of the case. Such facts constitute the
basis of all reasoning on the subject. I therefore
now proceed to lay before the reader the following *facts*,
reasonings, and *suggestions*, which I commend to the
thoughtful and prayerful attention of all such as
desire to arrive at well-founded convictions in
reference to the matter before us.

The excellency of our Authorised Translation is
universally admitted. Who can deny that this
superiority is due, in great measure, to the fact,
that in it we have the result of successive revision?
To treat with some fullness this part of the subject,
it may be well to trace the history of the Version
used in the Western Church. One of the most
ancient, and, for the New Testament, the most
valuable Translation, has been well-named by critics
the "Ante-Hieronymian," or "Version before Jerome."
It is the same which used to be less properly
designated "The Italic." The Old Testament part
was merely a version of the Septuagint (or Greek
translation), and is therefore of only secondary importance. The New Testament part was unquestionably made from the Original, and, probably, about
the middle of the Second century, or about 50 years
after the death of the Apostle John. In distinction
from the Vulgate Version, we may call it the "Old
Latin." It must have been made from Greek MSS.
older by about two centuries than any now known to
exist, and it therefore represents to us, in the way of

Translation, the most ancient text of the Greek Testament. Its value is inestimable, and one can hardly look upon it without a peculiar feeling of gratitude and reverence. No complete copy of it remains, but enough is extant to aid us in determining its character, and, in the case of disputed readings, its authority ranks very high indeed. The name of the translator is entirely unknown, but the style of the Version renders it almost certain that it was made in North Africa, inasmuch as it abounds in examples of a phraseology peculiar to the North-African writers. This continued to be the standard Translation for all Latin-speaking Christians until the time of Jerome. By that time the copies had become very much corrupted, and greatly differed from one another. Jerome, having translated the Old Testament from the Hebrew, slightly revised the Latin Translation of the New. The two together make up the present Vulgate. The Vulgate, (with the exception of the Psalms, which is mostly a Translation from the LXX.,) is made up of a translation, by Jerome, of the Old Testament, and a slight revision of the Latin New Testament previously in use.

We have therefore in the New Testament part of the Codex Amiatinus—(the most exact copy of the Vulgate as left by Jerome at present extant)—substantially the very Version of the Greek Scriptures which was read in North Africa, in the Second

century of the Christian era. The character of the
translator may, to some extent, be gathered from his
work. He must have been possessed of a fair knowledge both of Greek and Latin. His aim was
evidently not to exhibit his learning or eloquence,
but to exhibit a faithful representation of his original.
A close examination of this Ancient Version, and a
careful comparison of its renderings with the corresponding passages in the Greek, may serve, in a
remarkable manner, to illustrate the defectiveness of
the Latin language as compared with the other
classic tongue of antiquity. The effort to translate
from Greek into Latin may be likened to that of a
musician attempting to make some very inferior
instrument give forth the notes which another has
just elicited from a full-toned organ. Whether we
regard precision or copiousness, the language of
ancient Rome is very far inferior indeed to that of
ancient Greece; and therefore no Latin Version of the
New Testament can, in all respects, adequately represent the Original. The Translator, in such a case, must
be repeatedly impeded by being compelled to use a less
perfect medium of communication than that employed
by the inspired writers; and in the ancient Latin Version there occur repeated instances of defective
translation, originating in the imperfection of the
grammatical structure, and the limited vocabulary of
the Latin, as compared with the Greek. The revision
of the Old Latin Version by Jerome, was executed

about 384 A.D.; after that date, the older edition
and the revised continued both in use for a considerable period, until gradually the superiority of
the latter was universally acknowledged, and thus
the Old Latin gave place to that which, in general
terms, may be described as the work of Jerome.
Centuries before the Council of Trent, the Vulgate
had been the Standard Translation of the Scriptures
throughout the whole Western Church.

For about 1000 years that venerable version
held — throughout Christendom — almost supreme
authority: so that when, by the decree of the
Tridentine fathers in 1546, it was declared to be
the Authentic and Standard Version of the Catholic
Church, probably very few considered themselves as
chargeable with any disrespect to the original
Scriptures, or as introducing any innovation. So
completely was the Vulgate Translation spoken of as
emphatically the very Word of God, that in a work
published in 1498, a Roman Catholic theologian thus
comments upon the statement in Genesis i. 10;
"The gathering together of the waters called He
seas." The Latin term for seas is *"Maria."* On this
ground, the writer asks, "What is the gathering
together of the waters but the accumulation of all
graces into one place, that is, into the Virgin Mary?
(Maria.) But there is this distinction, that Maria (the
seas), has the (i) short, because that which the seas
contain is only of a transitory nature, while the gifts

and graces of the blessed Virgin (Maria) shall endure for ever."

This brief sketch of the history of the Vulgate may serve to show its claims to our regard. Its different portions indicate its different origin. It seems to me, with all deference to more qualified judges, that the more elegant and paraphrastic style of the Old Testament part corresponds with the historical fact of its being the work of Jerome; while the remarkable literality and peculiar phraseology of the New Testament serves to show how very slight were the alterations which the learned father thought it expedient to make upon the Version previously in use. Let any one read in his Greek Testament the 11th of Matthew, for example, and then peruse the same chapter, successively, in the old Latin, in the Vulgate, and in our Common Translation; and he will. be delighted to find a remarkable illustration of the foreseeing care of God over His own Word. All who will take the pains to make the experiment, will find that, substantially, the very same Gospels and Epistles, read in North Africa in the Second century of the Christian era, are now read in our own England, and throughout the whole world. During the prevalence of the Latin Vulgate in Europe, the Greek Testament was almost entirely unknown. Divine truth, originally given forth in Hebrew and Greek, had been for ages consigned to the keeping of a Latin Translation; and when, at the revival of learning, the originals became the subjects of earnest study, it was evident, that although many errors, more or less important, had crept into the copies of the Version, and some very serious mis-translations had from the first been retained in it, yet the essential truths set forth in the writings of prophets, evangelists, and apostles, were found to have been preserved in the Version, taken as a whole.

I have thus minutely dwelt upon the origin and history of the Vulgate, because of its very important bearing upon all the leading translations circulated in Modern Europe. Upon it, all the Roman Catholic Versions, in English or in other modern languages, are with very few exceptions, confessedly based; in fact, generally speaking, all such Versions are mere translations from that which is still regarded as the Authentic and Standard edition of the Scriptures in the Roman Catholic church. Its very great antiquity; its extensive and long-continued prevalence; the peculiarity and importance of some of the errors contained in it; the controversies connected with some of its mis-renderings; the influence which, whether directly, or by means of Modern Translations, it is even now exercising on the minds of vast numbers of nominal Christians—all combine to call the attention of Biblical scholars to its excellencies and defects. But few appear to me to be aware of the influence which, in all probability, the New Testament part, at least, must have exerted on the

Protestant Translations which have been published
since the era of the Reformation, in the several
countries of Europe, Asia, and America. Our own
Protestant Bible will be found to bear internal
evidence of the influence exerted by the Vulgate on
the minds of the early translators. Wycliffe's
Translation, as is well known, was not made from
the originals, but simply from the Latin. At the date
of its publication, about 1380, or nearly 1000 years
after Jerome's revision of the Old Latin, Hebrew and
Greek were unknown even to the most eminent
scholars and theologians in England; so that, if the
Scriptures were to be given to the people in the
vernacular language, it was absolutely necessary to
translate from the Vulgate. When Tyndale, about
the year 1525, published that Version of the New
Testament which was destined to be the basis of all
our leading Protestant Translations, it is true that he
took as the basis of his text the Greek Original. I
doubt whether, in any instance, he consciously
retained anything from the Vulgate, if not confirmed
by the Greek Text. His scholarship, his diligence,
his faith, courage, zeal, and purity of life, all
combined to render him, indeed, an instrument suited
for such a work; and, without desiring in any way to
disparage the claims of other labourers in the same
field, to Tyndale more than to any other single
individual, it appears to me we are indebted for the
inestimable gift of our English Bible. Still, although

his Version is derived not from the Latin, but, in the strictest sense, from the Greek, he must have been familiar from his youth with the Vulgate, and been thus led unconsciously to follow, in several instances, its interpretation of the meaning of the inspired writers.

Coverdale, Rogers, Cranmer, and even Parker and his coadjutors, were all, probably, more or less, under the same influence; so that, when the scholars appointed by King James to revise the Authorized Version, entered upon their arduous labours, they had before them several successive translations,—all more or less modified by the fact of their having been either executed, or edited, by Theologians who had been readers of the Vulgate, before they had acquired any acquaintance with the Greek Original. Even the Geneva Version,—although very distinct from the other translations already referred to,—was probably modified by the Latin in some instances. In John x. 16, where Tyndale had rightly given *"one flock and one shepherd,"* the Geneva of 1557 (followed by that of 1560), gives *"one sheep-fold and one shepherd."* The Bishop's Bible follows the Geneva, and hence our Authorized, to this day, retains the mistake. The origin of the error is found in the Latin *"ovile,"* " sheep-fold," instead of *"grex,"* "flock."

It is well for those who are interested in such subjects, to notice the order of succession, and the age of the several English Versions that were published previously to the date of our Authorized Bible.

L

Tyndale's first edition of the New Testament in 1525 was republished in a revised form in 1534. Coverdale published the whole Bible in 1537. Rogers (under the name of Matthews) published another edition about the same time. The Great Bible, a revision of that of Rogers, probably by Coverdale, appeared in 1539. Cranmer's,—very nearly the same as the last-mentioned,—was given to the world in 1540. One Geneva Version, probably by William Whittingham, was published in 1557, and may be regarded as preparatory to the Version by the Geneva Translators, published along with their Translation of the Old Testament, in 1560, which latter is to be regarded as "*The* Geneva Translation." The Bishop's Bible appeared in 1568, and continued to be the edition used in the churches, until it was superseded by that which, for about 250 years, has retained its place as the standard edition of the English Bible.

In the preparation of that edition, the revisers were required to retain the rendering of the Bishop's Bible in every case where faithfulness to the Original did not necessitate alteration; and, if alteration should be requisite, the needful correction was to be sought, in the first place, in some one of the former leading Protestant Translations. Only if those failed to furnish such correction were the revisers to act on their own responsibility. It is obvious that, under such limitations, they could hardly be regarded as *translators* in the ordinary sense of the word. They were, moreover, strictly required to retain the old Ecclesiastical terms.

Limited as they were by the regulations of their royal patron, they accomplished a work which has been the means of incalculable benefit to England and America, and the beneficial influence of which has been diffused over the whole world.

As we trust that their spirits have long been reposing in the paradise of God, so we would cherish on earth a reverential regard for their memory. It might have been well that they had been left at greater freedom, and that, in some respects, their work had more resembled a Re-translation; but, on the other hand, it is pleasant to think that thus, through our English Bible, we are linked to the martyrs of the Reformation, and that we read, substantially, the very Book on which Tyndale, Coverdale, and Rogers, expended their hours of sacred study. The men to whom we owe our English Translation were not mere scholars or theologians; they were giants in faith and devotedness to God. They counted not their lives dear unto them, so that they might finish their course with joy. They received as the reward of their toil, not the applause, but the opposition of their fellow-men. They had before them, not the prize of scholarship, but the crown of martyrdom. Tyndale, betrayed and condemned by his treacherous and cruel enemies, and unaided by those who ought to

have protected him, died by the hand of the
executioner in a foreign land, leaving behind him
a stainless and imperishable name. Rogers was the
first who suffered martyrdom in the Marian Persecution, and Miles Coverdale was permitted, at a
very advanced age, to experience the trials of poverty.
The very circumstances under which our English
Bible was translated, are fitted to endear it to our
hearts. As the original writers of the Gospels and
Epistles were exposed, while they wrote, to the perils
of fiery persecution, and were under no temptation to
follow cunningly devised fables, or to seek, by
adaptation to the popular taste, for reputation or
applause; so the translators of our Bible were not so
situated as to be influenced by worldly motives,
connected either with fame or outward distinction.
Their present reward consisted in the consciousness
of being engaged in doing the will of God, and in
benefitting their fellow-men; their ultimate reward
will be the crown of glory which fadeth not away,
bestowed on them in the great day of manifestation.

Surely every intelligent reader must perceive how
unfounded is the charge of innovation brought
against those who would advocate still further
revision, with a view to increasing the accuracy
of that which is already on the whole so faithful.
For nearly one hundred years the best scholars and
holiest men in England devoted their labours to the
improvement of our Translation, and that with

acknowledged success. Why should we refuse to cherish the hope that still further improvement would be the result of efforts made by the Christian scholars 'of our own day? During the long period that has passed away since the last revision, the Greek Language has been more carefully studied than at any former period; and, in respect of the minutiæ of Greek Grammar, modern scholars are far in advance of those who flourished in the early part of the Seventeenth century. Whether from defect of knowledge, or from laxity, or inattention, the early Translators have repeatedly failed in the exact renderings of the Greek Tenses, and in other points in regard to which modern scholars, whether in England or on the Continent, would not be likely to fall into similar mistakes.

During the last two centuries, and especially since the beginning of the present, immense stores of information have been accumulated, fitted, in various ways, to assist the diligent student of the Hebrew and Greek Scriptures. Not only have the original languages been more accurately studied, but much progress has been made in our acquaintance with the Antiquities, the Geography, the Botany, the Natural History, &c., of the Bible; and recent discoveries in Egypt, Assyria and Babylon have furnished helps for the better understanding and more correct translation of our Sacred Books. Surely it is desirable that all who are interested in the written

Word of God should be enabled to derive profit and instruction from the valuable results of so much laborious research and so many important discoveries.

But, besides the reasons obviously resulting from the present advanced state of Biblical scholarship, revision is requisite on other grounds.

Our last revisers left some manifest errors of their predecessors uncorrected; in some instances they altered for the worse; they retained, in other cases, terms now unintelligible to ordinary readers; they very frequently varied the rendering of Hebrew or Greek words without the slightest necessity, and have thus obscured the meaning of the sacred writers; on the other hand, they have sometimes represented by the same English word, terms which, in the Original, are used to express very distinct meanings.

There is one other weighty reason for seeking to improve our present Translation, to which I can only very briefly refer. The collection of ancient MSS. of the Hebrew and Greek Scriptures has led, in many instances, to the correction of the Original Text from which our Version was derived. Even those whose tendencies are most conservative must be constrained to admit that the Received Text, from which, for the most part our Translation was made, contains no small number of passages which a more exact acquaintance with the best authorities would require us to expunge, or modify, or correct. There are also some insertions for which the same authorities demand admission into the text. In regard to such alterations in the received Greek Text, prudence would require that they should be made with the greatest caution. It would be well that none should be allowed, but such as are warranted by the most satisfactory evidence; and, whether in the way of excision or addition, nothing should be done rashly, or without the concurrence of those critics best qualified to decide in points of so great delicacy and importance.

I now go on to produce some instances of antiquated terms, or erroneous or defective renderings in our English Bible, as fitted to illustrate the reasonableness and expediency of its being subjected to still further revision.

In Genesis xlv. 6, Joseph thus addresses his brethren:

"Yet there are five years in which ¦there shall be neither earing nor harvest."

Again in Exodus xxxiv. 21, a similar expression occurs:

"In earing time and in harvest thou shalt rest."

Repeatedly, in conversation with intelligent readers of the English Scriptures, I have found that the meaning of "earing time" was altogether misapprehended. Many being unacquainted with the old English verb "to ear,"—equivalent to the modern term "to plough," are led to connect the expression "earing" with ears of corn, and are thus entirely misled as to the period of the year intended. For "earing" we ought to substitute the modern word "ploughing."

A corresponding correction is required in the following passages:

"A rough valley which is neither eared nor sown." (Deut. xx. 4.)

ought to be read, "which has neither been ploughed nor sown."

"To ear his ground." (I. Samuel viii. 12.)

should be, "to plough his ground."

In Isaiah xxx. 24, the Hebrew term rendered "ear" in the clause:

"The young asses that ear the ground,"

is different from that occurring in the instances given above, but the meaning is nearly the same.

In II. Kings xxiii. 6, we find a statement which must have startled many a thoughtful reader:

"And he brought out the grove from the house of the LORD, without Jerusalem, unto the brook Kidron, and burned it at the brook Kidron, and stamped it small to powder, &c."

We read also, in II. Kings xvii. 10, and elsewhere, of "groves" being set up on every high hill and under every green tree.

Now, in such passages, no reader of ordinary understanding can fail to perceive that the word "groves" cannot possibly be taken in its usual signification. But still, he is left entirely to conjecture what meaning it is intended to convey.

In the above passages, and in many others where the word "grove," either in the singular or plural, is found in our Version, the Hebrew term is employed either as the name of the Syrian goddess Astarte, or is applied to images of that divinity, or perhaps, in some cases, to idolatrous images in general.

Thus in Judges iii. 7, we should read:

"The children of Israel did evil in the sight of the LORD, and forgat the Lord their God, and served Baalim and Asheroth," or the Baals and the Astartes, (*i.e.* the male and female divinities of their idolatrous neighbours.)

In Judges vi. 35, "the grove" should be "the image of Astarte," see also, verses 26, 28, 30.

In I. Kings xv. 13, Asa is said to have removed his mother, Maachah, from being queen,

" Because she had made an idol in a grove."

The correct rendering of the Hebrew conveys a very different piece of information, "because she had dedicated an image to Astarte," (or made an image of Astarte.)

In I. Kings xviii. 19:

" The prophets of the groves,"

ought to be "the prophets of Astarte."

II. Kings xiii. 6, for

"There remained the grove also in Samaria,"

read "and also the image of Astarte continued to stand in Samaria."

Correct in a similar way, II. Kings xvii. 16; xviii. 4; xxi. 3, &c. In verse 7, read "graven image of Astarte."

Similar alterations are required in the corresponding passages in II. Chronicles.

In II. Kings xxiii. 7, we have two mis-renderings in one brief clause.

" The women wove hangings for the grove,"

ought to read "the women wove shrines [lit: houses or receptacles], for Astarte." In this instance the one error evidently led to the other. A house, receptacle or shrine for a grove, was so incongruous an expression, that it was deemed absolutely needful to depart from the obvious signification of one of the simplest terms in the language. The application of the term for a house to a consecrated tent or shrine for an idol, is entirely in accordance with the nature of the case; the rendering "hangings," conveys either no meaning at all, or one totally inapposite; besides being without any philological warrant. In this instance, neither the LXX. nor the Vulgate furnish any sanction to the rendering "hangings." The Greek interpreters leave the Hebrew word untranslated, and insert a barbarous term which appears like a wrongly spelt representation of the original: the Vulgate renders "little houses," i.e., "receptacles" or "shrines." The Geneva Version of 1560, gives exactly the same words as those employed by our translators. In the margin of our Version we find the word "houses," which is the correct rendering of the Hebrew.

In Judges ix. 53, we read:

"And a certain woman cast a piece of a mill-stone upon Abimelech's head, and all to break his skull."

In other editions, more correctly printed, instead of of "break" we find "brake."

If read in the former way, the "to" is taken as the sign of the infinitive, and the clause must be understood as expressing only the purpose or intention of the woman. If, on the other hand, we find "brake" in our copy of the Bible, except we happen to be acquainted with the obsolete expression "all to," the passage will be quite unintelligible. Few readers are aware that "all to" is equivalent to "altogether," "entirely," "wholly." The verb in the Hebrew being in the intensitive form, expresses the completeness of the act. "She completely broke his scull." So the Vulgate, "et confregit cerebrum ejus." "And broke his scull in pieces." The Italian of Diodati, to the same purpose, "e gli spezzò il teschio," and the French of Ostervald, "et lui cassa le crâne." The Geneva (1560), gives "and brake his braine pan."

The obsolete expression "all to," occurs in Luke vii. 38, and xv. 20, as rendered in the Bishop's Bible of 1568.

In the former instance it is said of the woman, "And all to kissed his feet;"

in the latter place we find it applied to the father of the prodigal son,

"And all to kissed him."

In both cases, the object of the translators obviously was, to exhibit the intensity of the verb used in the Original. So utterly, however, has the old adverb fallen into disuse, that not one reader in a thousand would readily understand its meaning.

In Judges xv. 19, in connexion with the history of Samson, we read:

> "But God clave an hollow place that was in the jaw and there came water thereout; and, when he had drunk, his spirit came again, and he revived : wherefore he called the name thereof En-hakkore, which is in Lehi unto this day."

The term rendered "jaw," is precisely the same which is translated "Lehi" in the close of the verse, and ought to have been taken as the proper name of a place in both instances. This error is found both in LXX. and the Vulgate, and is reproduced in the Geneva Version. It is quite true that our translators have inserted "Lehi" in the margin, but very many Bibles are printed without the marginal readings. Even those who use the fuller editions, containing the readings in question, are very likely to pass them by without notice.

In Psalm xxii. 21, we read:

> "Save me from the lion's mouth : for Thou hast heard me from the horns of the unicorn."

This Version is unquestionably erroneous. The verse may bear either of the two following renderings:

"Save me from the lion's mouth, and hear me (*i.e.* deliver me) from the horns of the unicorns."

Or,

"Save me from the lion's mouth, and from the horns of the unicorns. Thou hast heard me, &c."

I could not give any full account of my reasons for preferring the latter of the two modes of rendering the verse, without entering into the minutiæ of Hebrew Grammar and accentuation. Either way is grammatically possible, but the whole connexion of the passage and the structure of the Psalm lead me to prefer the latter. When thus read, the words— "Thou hast heard me"—serve to divide the Psalm into two entirely distinct, yet closely connected, parts. From the commencement down to this triumphant utterance the language has been that of an afflicted suppliant, almost overwhelmed by the crushing weight of his sorrows, and the terrible fierceness of his enemies. In verse 22, there begins a strain of joyousness, gratitude, and praise. The delivered suppliant expresses His purpose to unfold to His brethren the character of that God unto whom He Himself had cried in the hour of His mysterious anguish, and from whom He had Himself experienced such complete deliverance.

For a period of twenty or thirty years I have been in the habit of so understanding the 21st verse of Psalm xxii. Only a few days ago, having consulted the Chaldee Targum on the Psalms, I found that the old Paraphrast had given the same version of the words. He gives—"Thou hast received my prayer."

Such are a very few specimens of passages in the Old Testament requiring alteration. Would the correction of such manifest mistakes, in any wise, deteriorate our English Bible? Would not the corrected copy be more adapted for edification than that in which so many similar instances of erroneous renderings are to be found? Does such an emendation as that to which the attention of the reader has just been directed effect nothing in the way of illustrating the structure and coherency of the Psalm? Can we honestly pray that we may enjoy the enlightening and quickening energy of the Holy Spirit, in enabling us to understand and enjoy His Word more fully, and yet remain indifferent as to the measure of accuracy with which our English Bible represents the meaning of the inspired writers? Surely it becomes those who, by the leadings of Divine providence, and, by mental taste and adaptation for such pursuits, have been induced to devote their best hours to the prayerful study of the Original Scriptures, to endeavour to turn their acquirements to profitable account, not merely, with a view to their own profit, but for the spiritual benefit of their fellow

Christians. Could I only be satisfied that I had the warrant of Him whom all true Christians worship as Head of His Church, I would gladly retire for a season from all other service, that, free from outward interruptions, I might carefully prepare a somewhat extended statement of those instances in which, I conscientiously believe, the Common Translation fails to represent the meaning conveyed by the Original. Such a work, if entered upon in a spirit of dependence and prayerful diligence, might be helpful, in some measure, to those who are unable to examine such passages, or to consult critical authorities for themselves. But, in so responsible an undertaking, two, or rather, as many qualified labourers as can be obtained, are better than one. Circumstances seem to forbid the prospect of a revision being undertaken at present, by authority. For that step the time is not yet come.

A voluntary association of Christian men belonging to different sections of the visible Church, and composed of such as have given satisfactory evidence of some measure of qualification for the work, might do far more than any single individual scholar acting on his own responsibility, and without the opportunity of being aided by friendly conference with others. The agreement of trustworthy revisers in the alterations proposed, would carry along with it great weight in the estimation of Christians in general.

Having referred to a very few, but not unimportant, examples of passages in the Old Testament requiring correction, I would further illustrate the necessity of revision, by reference to one or two mis-renderings in the New Testament.

I once asked an intelligent young man who was looking forward to being engaged in the Gospel ministry, whether all the Apostles were Jews by birth. He replied at once in the negative, and referred to the statement in the Gospel by Matthew, x. 4. There it is stated expressly that one of the twelve was Simon, the Canaanite. If our Translation is to be relied on, in this particular, then undoubtedly the negative answer was the correct one. But every reader of the Original knows that the term rendered "Canaanite," (in Matthew x. 4, and Mark iii. 18), is equivalent to the term "Zelotes," employed by Luke xi. 15. In Matthew and Mark, the Hebrew term for a Zealot (*i.e.* one belonging to the sect of the Zealots), is employed with a Greek termination; in Luke's Gospel, the Greek term is adopted. The meaning in all three is the same.

In Matthew xii. 40, "whale," ought to read "great fish." A translator ought not to aim at being more definite than the writer whose meaning he undertakes to represent. There is no authority for asserting that the whale was the species of fish to which the narrative refers.

In the account given of Herod's conduct towards John the Baptist, in Matthew xiv. 6, as compared with Mark vi. 24, there is an apparent discrepancy which is entirely due to a mis-translation in the narrative of the former. The term rendered "before instructed," ought to be translated "being instigated." It does not refer to any previous instruction by which the mother might have prepared the daughter to ask for the life of the distinguished prophet, but to the fact that, after the promise had been uttered by the King, Herodias asked direction from her mother as to the request. This erroneous translation is to be found in the Vulgate, and has kept its ground ever since. Tyndale reads,— evidently misled by the Latin "præmonita a matre,"— "being informed of her mother before." The Geneva, 1557, and also that of 1560, as well as the Bishop's Bible of 1568, agree with our own Version; or rather, our last Translators left the passage as they found it.

In Mark xxiii. 24, the term "strain," is generally mis-understood because of the accompanying preposition "at." "To strain," may mean either "to purify by filtration," or "to make violent efforts." The Greek term can only be used to express the former notion. Accordingly we find in Tyndale, in both Geneva Versions, and in the Bishop's Bible, "strain out." There is every reason for believing that the reading "strain at," in our Authorized Translation, is due to a mistake of the printer.

In I. Thessalonians, v. 22:

"Abstain from all appearance of evil,"

has been more correctly given in the Geneva, 1557,— "abstain from all kind of evil." I find "appearance" in the Geneva, 1560, and also in the Bishop's Bible. Our Translators are, therefore, not responsible for introducing this rendering, but only for leaving it uncorrected.

The same remark applies to John x. 16. Tyndale gives:

"And there shall be one flocke and one Shepherde."

The Geneva, 1557, altered "flocke" into "sheep-folde:" the Geneva, 1560, and the Bishop's Bible, 1568, retained the alteration, and our Translators left the rendering as they found it; while they ought to have restored the correct rendering given by Tyndale.

I may here remark, that an acquaintance with the previous Versions may often furnish considerable assistance in the detecting and correction of the errors that yet remain in our Authorized Translation. The Version of 1568—having been the basis of the present one—particularly deserves to be consulted, and yet I suspect it is less known, particularly in the New Testament part, than some of the others. Many derive their knowledge of the leading Trans-lations produced in the sixteenth century entirely from Bagster's Hexapla; but the plan of that very valuable work necessarily excluded the Geneva of 1560, and the very important Version of 1568. The Geneva of 1557, given in the Hexapla, is a Version of very great value, but it is entirely distinct from that of 1560. As an illustration of the distinction between the two, if the reader will take the trouble to compare the translation of Matthew xx. and xxi., as given in the Geneva of the Hexapla, with the same chapters as represented by the Geneva Translators in the edition of 1560, he will find that there are about eighty differences between them. Within the compass of those two chapters, the earlier Version retains 74 renderings from Tyndale, which are found altered in that of 1560.

I have reason to think that very many, accustomed to the use of the Hexapla, have received the impression that the second Geneva, published in 1560, along with the Old Testament, was merely a reprint of the former. It would be nearer the truth to represent the earlier Version as, in a good measure, a revised edition of Tyndale, and the second as almost a new Translation. The earlier one was probably the work of William Whittingham, and was only preparatory to the other, in which Whittingham was associated with several others of the exiles at Geneva. In the article "Versions," in Kitto's "Cyclopædia of Biblical Literature," the learned writer has inadvertently made a statement in relation to this matter contrary to fact. After referring to the Version of 1560, of which he says:—"The work is a new Translation from the Original, not simply a revision of any former Version. It is faithful and literal." He adds—"The new Testament portion was reprinted by Bagster in his Hexapla." A single glance at the top of the page containing the Geneva Version suffices to inform the reader that the reprint is from that of 1557.

In Acts xix. 37, the expression "robbers of churches" has been improperly retained in our English Bible. The Version of Tyndale, having been uncorrected, in this instance, in the Bishop's Bible, was allowed to remain; but the Geneva of 1560 would have furnished the more accurate rendering:

" Ye have brought hither these men which have neither committed sacrilege, neither do blaspheme your goddess."

The Rheims Version, in a similar way, had given the verse thus:

" For you have brought these men, being neither sacrilegious nor blaspheming your goddess."

The rendering of I. Timothy, vi. 2, as found in our Authorized Version, is wanting in accuracy and clearness. Every reader of the Greek Testament, familiar with the simplest rules respecting the use of the Greek article, will at once detect the mistake.

The English is scarcely intelligible: the Greek expresses the sense without the slightest ambiguity:—

"And they that have believing masters, let them not despise them because they are brethren ; but rather do them service, because those who receive the benefit are believers and beloved."

In this instance, had our Translators consulted the Vulgate or its representative, the Rheims Version, they would have found the more correct rendering ready to their hand.

In I. Timothy, v. 4, the term "nephew," in the sense of "grandchild" or other descendant, is likely to mislead ordinary readers, on a point of much practical importance. The obligation, however much it may morally and spiritually belong to other blood-relations, is expressly laid, not upon nephews, but upon connexions in the direct line of descent. In this case the early Versions appear to have guided the Revisers of 1611: the term "nephew" being formerly used in the sense of "grandson." It is so used by Hooker—the eloquent author of "The Ecclesiastical Polity,"—who died just a little before King James I. ascended the throne. It may safely be affirmed that not one reader out of a thousand is aware of the word having changed its meaning, inasmuch as it is never used in its former signification by those who speak or write modern English.

Among the many examples of carelessness in attending to the force of the article, we may instance I. Timothy, vi. 5. The Apostle, describing the characteristics of certain false teachers, asserts that they are—

"Men of corrupt minds and destitute of the truth, supposing that godliness is gain," (not "gain is godliness.")

i.e. regarding godliness as a means of promoting their own temporal advantage. In this instance, Tyndale, the Geneva of 1557 and 1560, the Bishop's Bible, and the Rheims Version, agree in disregarding the article, and consequently misrepresenting the meaning.

In Luke xiv. 8, 10, "room," ought to be altered into "place." The term "conversation," which is of such frequent occurrence in the Scriptures, is never used in the modern sense of the word, but almost always as denoting "conduct," deportment," "behaviour," or "general course of life." It is found only twice in the Old Testament, viz., Psalm xxxvii. 14, and Psalm l. 23, and answers to the Hebrew "derek" in the sense of "way," as given in the margin. In I. Peter, iii. 1, I suspect that many readers understand the Apostle as employing the word "conversation," in the modern sense of "familiar intercourse." There can be no question that the "behaviour," or "habitual conduct" of the wife, is that to which the sacred writer refers. In Philippians iii. 20, the Greek word rendered "conversation" denotes "citizenship," or rather "commonwealth," or "polity."

The rendering "conversation" in the above passage was introduced by Tyndale, and retained by those that followed him.

In Hebrews xiii. 5, the word so rendered is entirely different from the term elsewhere translated "conversation;" and appears to me to denote rather "disposition" or "turn of mind;" although also capable of designating the "course of life," or "habitual behaviour."

In Romans vi. there are several instances of inattention to the proper translation of the tenses. Thus, verse 2,

"We that are dead to sin,"

should be "we that died to sin."

Again, verse 4, read "we were buried with Him:" and in verse 6, read "our old man was crucified with Him, &c."

The last clause of II. Cor. v. 14, should be rendered, "if one died for all, then all died."

So also Gal. ii. 20, "if righteousness come by the law, then Christ died in vain."

To one whose hopes are all based on the fact that Christ has been raised from the dead, and who habitually thinks of the Saviour as the living Intercessor, ever carrying on His priestly advocacy within the Holiest of all on behalf of His people, there is something jarring in the assertion "Christ is dead." The Greek says no such thing, but merely asserts the fact that "He died."

In Hebrews x. 34, the correct reading of the Greek requires the following alteration in the Version, "knowing that ye have for yourselves a better and an enduring substance in heaven." The Greek ἐν = *in*, is an Interpolation rejected by all the best authorities. Here the change, or rather omission, of one little word makes a very considerable difference in the meaning of the passage.

In I. Peter iii. 15,

> "Sanctify the Lord God in your hearts,"

we should read "the Lord Christ." Thus amended, according to the most ancient MSS., we find that Christ, in the mind of Peter, answers to Jehovah in Isaiah. See Isaiah viii. 13, 14, compared with I. Peter ii. 8.

In Rev. xxii. 14, there is strong ground for rejecting—

> "They that do His commandments,"

and for adopting the reading, "Blessed are they that wash their robes." The Rhemish Version gives, according to the Vulgate, "Blessed are they that wash their stoles." In the modern editions, the antiquated term "stoles" is exchanged for "robes." The most ancient Greek MS. of the Revelation supports the reading of the Vulgate.

I would earnestly seek to impress upon the minds of my readers, that the exact translation of the Holy

Scriptures is not a matter which concerns only critics and theologians. The mis-rendering of a simple term may serve very grievously to mislead those who cannot refer to the Original; in other words, may serve to convey a wrong impression to the overwhelming majority of Christians in our country. The Greek term rendered "Take no thought," in Matthew vi. 25, may lead to fanaticism on the one hand, and to false principles of interpretation on the other. He who believes that Christ really meant that His disciples should "take no thought" respecting the things of this life, will be in great danger of dishonouring the cause of truth by carelessness about his worldly concerns; or, on pretence that the words of our Lord cannot be received in their obvious meaning, will be tempted, by lax interpretation, to blunt the edge of those precepts which the Great Teacher has left for our direction.

"Be not anxious about your life,"

conveys a very different idea from that which, in our modern English, would be understood by the rendering of our Translators. In verses 27, 28, 31, 34, and x. 19; also in Luke x. 41; xii. 11, 22, 25, 26; and Philip. iv. 6, a similar correction is required.

In Hebrews x. 23, by a manifest oversight, our last Translators have substituted,

"Let us hold fast the profession of *our* faith,"

for the correct reading of the previous Versions.

" The profession of *our* faith," ought to have been "the profession of *our* hope," or rather, as in the Bishop's Bible, "the hope." I am not aware that the error of our Authorized Translation, in this instance, is to be found in any Version in any language of the world. No Greek MS. and no Ancient Version sanctions the substitution of the one term for the other.

A minute attention to the exact force of the terms employed in the Original will sometimes throw considerable light upon passages, the import of which has been much controverted.

In John iii. 9, we find it asserted respecting every one who is born of God,

> " He cannot sin."

Now this expression might, in English, represent two very different statements. The words are, literally, "he is not able to sin." Had "to sin" been expressed by the Aorist infinitive, the meaning would have been, "he cannot sin in one single instance," or "he is not able to sin at all." The infinitive being in the present tense, the meaning, according to the idiom of the language, might be represented in English, thus:

> " He is not able to be sinning," (*i. e.* he cannot go on in a course of sin.)

In the same Epistle, ii. 1,

> " If any man sin, we have an advocate, &c."

might have been so expressed, as to imply habitual

sinning. Such a statement would have been contrary to the whole character of Scripture teaching. But here the verb is in the subjunctive Aorist, and is to be thus translated—"if any man have sinned," or as the Vulgate admirably gives it, "Si quis peccaverit."

In the petition for our daily bread, contained in the prayer which our Lord taught His disciples, the verb "give," in Matthew, does not exactly correspond in tense to that which is translated "give," in the Gospel of Luke. In Matthew vi. 11, we read rightly,

"Give us this day our daily bread."

The Aorist imperative is used with reference to one particular instance, the immediate reference being only to "this day." But in Luke xi. 3,

"Give us day by day our daily bread,"

a moment's reflection leads us to observe that the verb "give," expresses not a transient, but a continuous act; and accordingly, it is put in the Aorist present, and literally rendered, would be thus represented, "Be thou giving us, day by day, our daily bread." The petition, as expressed in Luke, is of larger application than as it stands in Matthew.

The instances just given from the Epistle of John and the Lord's Prayer, as recorded in the Gospels, are of a different character from those examples of mistranslation designed to illustrate the need of revision. The three last instances may serve to illustrate the precision of the Greek language, and the advantages of studying the Original Scriptures; but the idiom of our own tongue would hardly bear any other rendering than that which we find in our Translation.

By a careful revision a considerable number of blemishes might be removed from our venerable Version, but no Translation can ever be a perfect and adequate representation of any work written in Hebrew, Greek, or Latin. Perhaps no ancient books are so susceptible of being well translated, as are those writings which make up the Old and New Testaments. Still, as all translators of Homer and Horace must utterly fail in adequately representing the sublime simplicity of the former, or the exquisite diction of the latter, so no translator, however highly gifted, can transfuse into any modern tongue, the full force, expressiveness, and energy of the words of Inspiration. Precious to all believing hearts, as are the Psalms of David, no Translation ever fully expressed all that which they convey to the reader of the Original; and although all men of literary taste have done homage to the poetic grandeur and touching pathos by which the Book of Job is characterized, perhaps not a single chapter, from the third to the close, has ever been exactly represented in any ancient or modern Version.

Before the great work of revising our English Bible be actually entered on, it would be well that a far larger number of intelligent Christians were stirred up to devote themselves to the study of the Original

Scriptures. In proportion as good men found, by experience, the benefit of more exact acquaintance with the records of inspiration, so would they become interested in seeking the removal of all really important errors from our English Version. Were the more intelligent members of our several Christian communities only alive to the desirableness of a revision being made, and aware of the difficulty of the task, the knowledge of the true state of the case would not only awaken interest, but call forth prayer. To Him "from whom cometh down every good and perfect gift," must we look for qualified labourers for such an arduous service. We have many devoted students of Scripture,—many eminent for learning and disposed for work; but I question whether there are to be found in England an adequate number of Christian scholars on whom the task might hopefully be devolved. To competent learning, critical skill, sound judgment, acquaintance with the leading Ancient and Modern Versions, and other secondary qualifications, there must be added others of a still higher character. Those who might safely be trusted with such a task, must be imbued with that loving reverence for the Scriptures, and that lowly submission to the truths therein taught, which can only be found in regenerated hearts. They must resolve to begin, carry on, and complete their labours in a spirit of habitual dependence and earnest prayer. It must be to them, emphatically, a labour of love.

The toil connected with the service must be lightened by the delight they find in being so employed. They must look continually to God for direction, and strength, and success in their undertaking, and expect not from man, but from the Master Himself, the reward of their labour. They must watch incessantly against every doctrinal or sectarian bias, and seek to acquit themselves as those who must give an account. Well may we exclaim, as we ponder over the magnitude and the difficulty of the task, and think how many influences are at work to hinder or to mar it—Are we warranted to expect its accomplishment? As we reflect, moreover, on the variety of endowments that would be needed for its execution, we are led to ask, "Who is sufficient for these things?

But surely, the God of all grace has exhaustless resources; and if it be for His glory and the good of His people, that the work should be effected, He will raise up suitable workmen, and impart to them all needful aid for the accomplishment of His will concerning it.

In the mean time, while the number of those who are seeking to acquaint themselves with the original languages of Scripture will, it is to be hoped, be continually increasing, it is at the same time desirable, that those who are only slightly conversant with such studies, should abstain from proposing, in public, any emendations on our received Translations, except such emendations be sanctioned by competent scholars. It is to be regretted that good men whose knowledge of Greek is of the most limited description should take it upon them to correct our translators on their own responsibility. It is, perhaps, still more hazardous for those who have acquired only a smattering of Hebrew to attempt the improvement of the English Old Testament. Corrections are needed both in the Old and New Testaments, but no mere school-boy acquaintance with the ancient languages is sufficient to constitute a Biblical critic. The cause of Bible revision has been brought into disrepute by rashness and officious intermeddling on the part of incompetent correctors.

In conclusion, I would desire to remind the reader how unanimous is the decision of all competent judges in relation to the very great excellence of our Authorized Translation. Taken as a whole, it is altogether superior to the LXX. or the Vulgate; while the two latter may often be of service in correcting, in particular instances, the errors of our Version. So marked is the superiority of our English Translation over those of antiquity, that the most learned of the fathers, if unable to refer to the Hebrew, were in a far less favourable position for understanding the Old Testament than any English Christian who is acquainted merely with his own mother tongue. Let any one examine the Exposition of the Psalms, by Augustine, and he will find proofs, without number, of the grievous mis-apprehensions resulting out of the very imperfect and erroneous Version used by that devout and eloquent expositor. The LXX. Translation of the Book of Psalms abounds with intolerable blunders; and the Latin Version of that part of Scripture is almost entirely according to the Greek. The Prayer-Book Version, taken from Cranmer's Bible, of 1540, is a very great improvement upon the Vulgate; while the Version of 1611 is again still nearer the Original.

There are a considerable number of corrections required in our Authorized Psalter of 1611; there are many more needed in that of 1640; but in the Vulgate and LXX. Psalter, the errors are not only exceedingly numerous, but often of the most intolerable character. The translation of the Pentateuch in the Greek Version is, on the whole, faithful and good. The translation of the Psalms is very carelessly executed. It is therefore much to be regretted, that while the rest of the Vulgate Old Testament is Jerome's Translation of the Hebrew, the Version of the Psalms, still retained in that venerable Latin Translation, should be almost entirely from the very erroneous Greek of the LXX.

Should any one be led to inquire into the distinctive difference between our own Version and that of Jerome, let him read a few chapters in the Douay Bible, and compare them with the same chapters as given in our own. The comparison will be still more satisfactory if he can read the Latin, of which the Douay professes to be a Version.

In Ecclesiastes i. 15, he finds in our Translation,

> " That which is crooked cannot be made straight
> And that which is wanting cannot be numbered."

This is a fair rendering of the Hebrew; but if he turns to the Vulgate, he reads:

> "Perversi difficile corriguntur,
> Et stultorum infinitus est numerus ;"

rightly rendered in the Douay Bible,

> " The perverse are hard to be corrected,
> And the number of fools is infinite."

This is a paraphrase, and not a translation, and may serve to illustrate the remarks previously made on the paraphrastic style of Jerome's Version of the Old Testament.

Thus, let any careful reader compare the history of Joseph as given in the Vulgate, with the same chapters in our English Bible, and he will not fail to be struck with repeated instances of the marked difference between the simplicity of the narrative, as given by the latter, and the ornate and paraphrastic mode of expression by which the former is characterized.

In Genesis xliv. 18, the word "boldly," is introduced without any warrant whatever from the Original. In verse 20,

> " Whose brother is dead,"

N

becomes, in the Vulgate, "whose uterine brother is dead."

"We said,"

in verse 22, becomes "we suggested," in the language of Jerome.

In Ruth i. 19,

"All the city was moved about them,"

is rendered, "The report was quickly spread among all."

Such instances are not given as examples of positively erroneous translation, but as fitted to illustrate the difference between the style and manner of the Vulgate, and the mode of expression employed by our own Translators.

The Latin Version is generally acknowledged to be, at least in the historical part of the Old Testament, a good and faithful Translation. The same terms of commendation may, without the slightest hesitation, be applied to the Authorised Version of the Hebrew Scriptures.

But in addition to the general characteristic of faithfulness, the latter deserves to be held in the very highest estimation for certain qualities peculiarly its own.

Our Translation not only conveys the meaning of the Original, but so conveys that meaning as to make upon the mind of the reader an impression very similar to that which is made by the reading of the

Hebrew. The Vulgate has failed to catch the spirit and manner of the inspired writers, even when it succeeds in expressing, with general accuracy, their statements or instructions; while our venerable Version retains their simplicity, impressive seriousness, dignity, and tenderness. Let any thoughtful reader make the experiment, and he will find that, for devotional reading, for quiet, meditative perusal of the Scriptures, neither the Greek of the LXX., nor the Latin of Jerome, will supply the place of his English Scriptures. I grant that the difference may arise, in some measure, from the fact that the English Bible has been familiar to most of us from our childhood, and is therefore connected with some of the tenderest and the strongest of our earliest associations. Still, apart from such claims upon our reverence and affection, the English Bible possesses excellencies inherent in its structure, and such as may be illustrated by comparison with other faithful Translations.

In Genesis xlii. 36, we read, in our Version:
"Joseph is not, and Simeon is not, and ye will take
    Benjamin away."
This is an unadorned, unaltered representation of the actual words employed by the patriarch. Every reader of taste perceives how the very exaggeration respecting Simeon, is in exact accordance with the state of the old man's feelings, as produced by successive strokes of overwhelming sorrow. A father

depressed as Jacob was would not be likely to weigh exactly the import of every word employed, or to watch against saying anything more than the literal truth. The naturalness and unaffected character of the whole description, has been reproduced by our translators, not through the aid of art or effort, but by simply retaining the phraseology of the Original. Let the reader now turn to the Vulgate, and observe the rendering given by Jerome:

"Joseph non est super, Simeon tenetur in vinculis, et Benjamin conferetis."

"Joseph is no more, Simeon is kept in bonds, and Benjamin ye will take away."

In this instance the learned Father assumes the position of a corrector, instead of a translator. He evidently aims to make the patriarch's assertion more in exact accordance with the facts of the case; but, in doing so, he is himself guilty of inaccuracy in the rendering of the clause.

It ought to be observed, that there is a far closer correspondency between the Hebrew and English languages, than between the Hebrew and the Latin. This gave our Translators a great advantage over Jerome. In addition to this, I think there can be very little question that the former had imbibed far more of the Spirit of the Book on which they were occupied, than the latter appears to have done.

Of all the leading Christian teachers in the early church, Jerome was by far the most distinguished for that sort of learning which relates to Biblical interpretation. But in depth of Christian experience, as well as in certain intellectual and moral qualities, he was far inferior to Augustine. It would have been well for himself and for the church, if to his vast erudition, marvellous diligence, and untiring zeal, he had added the graces of Christian simplicity, and graciousness of temper. When we compare his attainments in the Christian life with those of our earliest translator, Tyndale, we find no difficulty in accounting for the superiority of our English Translation over that of Jerome, in all such qualities as depend upon the *spiritual condition* of the respective Authors.

On the whole, it will be all but universally admitted, at least by Protestant scholars, that our Common Version is very much nearer perfection than that which was declared by the Council of Trent, to be the Authentic and Standard Translation of the Roman Catholic Church. No Protestant Version contains such blunders as the following:—Exodus xxxiv. 29, &c., where it is said of Moses,

> " He knew not that his face was horned :"

and verse 30,

> " And Aaron and the children of Israel, seeing the face of Moses horned, were afraid to come near."

In Psalm i. 1,

"The seat of the scorners,"

is rendered "the chair of pestilence." And in Psalm ii. 12, for

"Kiss the Son lest He be angry,"

we find, "embrace discipline lest, at any time, the Lord be angry." In Psalm cxxvi. 4, instead of

"Children of youth,"

we find, "the children of them that have been shaken."

Such are some of the positive mis-renderings of the Vulgate. They abound in the Psalms,— the Version of that · part of the Old Testament being, as formerly noticed, a re-production of the very erroneous Version of the LXX. But very frequent mis-translations are found also in the Book of Proverbs, for which Jerome must be held responsible.

The Latin Version, so long the only Bible of the Western Church, has been too highly commended by Romanists, and too much disparaged by Protestant Theologians. It is inferior in correctness to most Translations of modern date, but the charges of Romanist teaching, and wilful perversion of the truth, have never been satisfactorily established. Its style has been denounced as barbarous, I venture to submit, on very insufficient grounds. There are instances without number, in which the classical idiom is violated, but no translator of the Hebrew Scriptures could have employed the style of Cicero or Livy, without running the risk of a more serious evil than that of inelegant phraseology.

Jerome must have been, from his familiarity with the writers of the purest Latinity, well qualified to write his own language with idiomatic elegance; but faithfulness to his original might have been sacrificed, had he attempted to express every Hebrew sentence in correct Latin phraseology.

In spite of the blemishes which mar the excellence of his work, and notwithstanding the faults of another kind which impaired the consistency of his Christian character, it becomes us to imitate his zeal in the study of Holy Scripture, and to venerate his memory as of one to whom, both from the Ancient and the Modern Church, a debt of gratitude is due.

In conclusion, let me sum up very briefly the convictions I have formed, and the course which I would recommend, in reference to the revision of our venerable Translation.

A nobleman, on succeeding to his paternal domains, may find that the old family castle, where for centuries his ancestors have dwelt,— although of noble structure and venerable aspect, requires some slight repairs and alterations, in order to render it a more convenient residence. Some of his friends may advise him to pull it down, and to build in its stead a modern mansion more suited to the taste of the present day; others may warn him against the slightest attempt to improve the venerable dwelling-place, even though, in some parts, the stones may have given way, and some portions of the building may have become unfit for use ; but those will give the best counsel, who advise him to preserve the ancient structure in all its integrity, and yet to make such slight alterations as will tend to improve its usefulness, without impairing its strength, or defacing its form.

So would I advise in reference to our English Bible. Let it be revised in a spirit of devout reverence and watchful caution. Let nothing be altered without valid reasons; but at the same time, let those words and phrases which are become altogether antiquated, and consequently unintelligible to ordinary readers, be exchanged for the corresponding expressions in modern English; and let manifest mis-translations be corrected. A revision thus conducted, not in a spirit of wanton innovation, but under a sense of responsibility to God, and with an upright purpose to glorify His name, could not fail to benefit the Church.

So far from detracting from the excellence of that Book which all English Christians so highly prize, such a revision would still more serve to endear it to our hearts, inasmuch as it would thus become an instrument still better adapted "for teaching, for conviction, for correction, for discipline in righteousness, that the man of God may be perfect, thoroughly furnished unto every good work."

PASSAGES OF SCRIPTURE EXPLAINED OR ILLUSTRATED IN THIS WORK.

OLD TESTAMENT.

O

NEW TESTAMENT.